SMACKED

RANDOM HOUSE
NEW YORK

SMACKED

A Story of White-Collar Ambition,
Addiction, and Tragedy

EILENE ZIMMERMAN

Published in the United States by Random House, an imprint and division of Penguin Random House LLC, New York.

RANDOM HOUSE and the HOUSE colophon are registered trademarks of Penguin Random House LLC.

Brief portions of this work were originally published in different form in "The Lawyer, the Addict," by Eilene Zimmerman (*The New York Times*, July 15, 2017).

Grateful acknowledgment is made to W. W. Norton & Company, Inc., for permission to reprint fourteen lines from "What the Living Do" from *What the Living Do* by Marie Howe, copyright © 1997 by Marie Howe. Used by permission of W. W. Norton & Company, Inc.

LIBRARY OF CONGRESS CATALOGING-IN-PUBLICATION DATA
Names: Zimmerman, Eilene, author.
Title: Smacked; a story of white-collar ambition, addiction, and tragedy / Eilene Zimmerman.
Description: First edition. |New York : Random House, [2020] | Includes bibliographical references. |
Identifiers: LCCN 2019029770 (print) | LCCN 2019029771 (ebook) | ISBN 9780525511007 (hardcover) | ISBN 9780525511014 (ebook)
Subjects: LCSH: Zimmerman, Eilene. | Zimmerman, Peter. | Lawyers—Drug use—United States. | Drug addiction—United States. | Drug addicts—United States—Biography. | White collar workers—Drug use—United States. | Workaholism—United States. | Divorced people—United States—Biography. | Grief.
Classification: LCC HV5824.L38 Z46 2020 (print) | LCC HV5824.L38 (ebook) | DDC 362.29092/2 [B]—dc23
LC record available at https://lccn.loc.gov/2019029770
LC ebook record availabl at https://lccn.loc.gov/2019029771

Printed in the United States of America on acid-free paper

randomhousebooks.com

987654321

First Edition

FOR MY CHILDREN AND FOR PETER

This is it.

Parking. Slamming the car door shut in the cold. What you called
    that yearning.

What you finally gave up. We want the spring to come and the
    winter to pass. We want
whoever to call or not call, a letter, a kiss—we want more and
    more and more and then more of it.

But there are moments, walking, when I catch a glimpse of myself
    in the window glass,
say, the window of the corner video store, and I'm gripped by a cherishing
    so deep

for my own blowing hair, chapped face, and unbuttoned coat
    that I'm speechless:

I am living, I remember you.

—FROM "WHAT THE LIVING DO," BY MARIE HOWE

■ PROLOGUE

July 11, 2015

I PLUG IN THE code to the gate at Peter's house and the door swings open to an expansive, rectangular backyard. The grass is mostly brown, the $20,000 fountain in the center no longer burbling, its white stones covered in algae. I go to the front door and put my key in the lock. It's made of heavy glass and makes a whooshing sound as it opens, like the door to an office building.

There's a staircase immediately in front of me that leads to the main floor, and to my right is the only room downstairs. It was intended to be a family or rec room, and has a glass wall facing the yard. I always thought it would be a great place for a party. Now it's been converted to a bedroom for our daughter, Anna, who is home from college for the summer. She stays here at her dad's house a few nights a week. Down here she has more independence, as well as her own bathroom. The bed is unmade, clothes and a bath towel litter the floor. Anna hasn't been here in two days. Neither has our son, Evan.

I hate the smell of this house. It's the smell of Peter, the smell of our divorce and all the heartache that came with it. His affair, his lies, his law career with its enormous pressure and salary and all the expensive things he buys with it. I also smell my own fear—of his relationships with various women, of his family life with our children, a life in which I'm no longer involved. It's the smell of Southern California and the ocean half a mile away, an expensive, privileged smell, but musty, too, like the inside of a refrigerator that hasn't been opened in a while.

I always feel like an intruder here. It's clear this isn't my house. Mine is a one-floor, mid-century home near the state university.

I call out, "Peter?" No answer, no sounds from upstairs. "Peter, are you here?" I climb the stairs to the main floor. It's perfectly quiet and still. I take a minute to look around. The house is an architectural trophy, made of steel, wood, and glass, all sharp angles and sunlight. Through the windows I can just make out a white line of sea-foam hitting the beach. I turn toward the kitchen. On the counter immediately to my right, Peter has set up a 25-inch digital frame displaying a series of family photos, him and our children. The images play in an endless, silent loop. There is also a large, nearly empty take-out soda, the kind you get at a convenience store, and some candy wrappers on the counter, piles of work papers, an asthma inhalator.

Peter has been sick for more than a year with some kind of ongoing, low-grade flu, constantly exhausted and weak. He's lost thirty pounds, maybe more, since we split up five years ago. But in the last six months, it's gotten worse. My kids say he sleeps the whole weekend when they are here, forgets to grocery shop, never makes meals. He doesn't seem to be going into the office much. The last time Anna and Evan were here, two days ago, their dad could barely lift his head off the pillow. Evan tried to take him to the hospital, but Peter refused, got angry and snapped at him.

Then he vomited onto the bedroom floor, threw a washcloth over it, and went back to bed.

I turn back to survey the loft-like living area, with a kitchen that morphs into a dining area that morphs into a living room, all of it filled with stylish modern furniture. The long table made from one piece of wood, splits and knots included, surrounded by six white leather and metal chairs. A side wall is covered in wallpaper that depicts trees in winter, gray renderings of trunks and branches against a white background.

No one has been able to reach Peter since Thursday morning, when Anna and Evan left to come back to my house. What if they are exaggerating? What if he's just sleeping? Or not here at all and I've just let myself into his house without permission? I have come here to check on him, to make sure he's okay and take care of him if he isn't.

I turn down the hallway where the bedrooms are located. "Peter?" I call again. "Peter, I'm coming down the hall to your bedroom, okay?" His bedroom is at the end of the hallway. Its door faces me and it's open, but I can't see anything except a corner of the bed and a cluttered night table. I walk past my son's bedroom, with its one orange wall and IKEA bed, past Anna's old bedroom, one wall painted deep pink and another wallpapered in a forest of black trees with little blackbirds resting on branches. Someone has cut out a silhouette of a rat and pasted it onto a branch.

I am nearly at his door and start calling his name again in earnest: "Peter? Peter?" I can see into the room. "I'm coming into your room, Peter. I'm here to check on you." The covers on his bed are drawn back, and I can see the crumpled white sheets. There are a few tissues in the bed, with spots of blood on them. I'm starting to shake badly as I walk into the bedroom.

Peter isn't in the bed, so I turn toward the master bath. Then

I see him, lying faceup on the floor between the bathroom and the bedroom.

I stand there, unable to really understand what I'm seeing. My mind is struggling to comprehend this. That's him? What's that on his face? There's a cardboard box under his head like a pillow. I walk over and kneel down next to him. His right arm is bent at the elbow and resting on his chest, a gesture he often makes, even when he is standing up. He holds his arm that way when he is making a point, pressing his thumb and first two fingers together for emphasis. Our son does the same thing.

I touch Peter's arms to shake him awake. They are stiff and hard to move. His fingernails are blue. I put my hand on his chest to try and feel his heart. I suddenly remember lying in our bed when we were married, spooning, my chest up against his back, especially when I was cold or couldn't sleep. I would listen for his heartbeat—so much slower and stronger than mine—and feel safe. Now I feel nothing. His chest is like unfinished wood, stiff, dry. And still. Is he dead? I don't know what a dead person looks like, so I tell myself that maybe he's unconscious. Maybe he needs CPR.

Then I look up at his face. There is a dried, black crust over most of it. His mouth is open slightly, the lips pulled back, a clear foamy fluid around the teeth. "Peter?" I say. I am crying, begging. "Peter?" Then I look at his eyes. They are open but something is wrong. At first, I can't figure it out but then I realize, slowly, what it is. His eyes have risen out of their sockets. No one alive has eyes like that, of this I am sure. I start screaming "ohmygod ohmygod" over and over again while I dig the phone out of my purse.

My hands are shaking so badly that I have to set the phone down on a table and use the speaker. I press 9, 1, 1 and hit the little green button. "I'm at the house of my ex-husband and I think he's . . . I think he died. Oh my god. I think he is dead." The woman on the other end sounds unmoved. "Ma'am, we can't help you if you don't calm down. Can you give me the address where you are right now?" I go outside and read it off the house because suddenly I can't remember it. "Ma'am, are you sure he's dead?" asks the 911 operator. I second-guess myself. What do I know about death? Maybe a person's eyes can look like that but they can still be saved, defibrillated or CPR-ed back to life? I agree to go back in and start chest compressions.

"I'll stay on the phone and guide you through it," the 911 woman says. "Okay, okay," I say, shaking and shivering. "I can't look at his face, though, I can't go near his face." The operator says, "That's fine, don't look at it." She tells me to move Peter's hand away from his chest. I pull gently, then harder. "I . . . I can't. It's, oh my god," I sob. "It's stiff. It's really stiff." The operator says, "Okay, don't worry about it. The police and ambulance will be there in about four minutes." I ask if she will stay on the line with me until they arrive. As I leave the bathroom I notice a small bloody hole below Peter's elbow. That's odd, I think. Then I run downstairs and out the front door to wait for help.

The shock of what is happening is starting to grow roots inside me. I can't keep still. I am a bundle of live wires—jittery and shooting hysterical sparks—and yet, at the same time, all business. I have the phone pressed to the side of my head, the 911 operator waiting with me for the police. I'm crying. Two boys on skateboards come down the street. They stop and hop down from their boards, one foot off, one foot on. The taller one asks, "Are you okay?"

It is a spectacular summer day, the sky deep blue and cloudless, a slight breeze off the ocean. And these two beautiful blond boys are having fun, just skateboarding down their street like they probably do every Saturday morning in San Diego, the land of endless summers. I want to tell them the whole world changed ten minutes ago, but instead I say, "Something happened to my ex-husband. He lives here. An ambulance is coming."

PART I

■ ONE
April 1987

IT'S A WARM SPRING afternoon and I am riding the 165 bus from northern New Jersey into midtown Manhattan, a long and nauseating drive. I'm heading to an appointment with a recruiter named Peter at Adam Personnel on 44th Street, in the hope he can help me find a job. A few months earlier I was laid off from my first post-college job, as an administrative assistant at CBS News in the Election & Survey Unit. The domino effect was swift. Not being able to pay rent meant leaving the apartment a friend and I had been renting near my alma mater, Rutgers University, and moving back to my mother's house in northern New Jersey. I'm depressed, I'm broke, and I'm cocktailing a few nights a week at a bar called The Orange Lantern, where I've also been going out with an over-muscled bartender who drives a Trans Am. I'm sleeping in my childhood bedroom and everything feels like 1975 instead of 1987—the mustard-colored walls, the gold and brown shag carpeting. I hope this recruiter can help me find a job, maybe even one that requires some writing.

My previous position at CBS News, ironically, involved no writing. During my year there, I climbed in rank from receptionist to administrative assistant, which raised my pay from $6.75 an hour to salaried staffer earning $18,000 a year and five minutes of television fame when I answered the "Decision Desk" phone on camera during the midterm-elections broadcast. At the conclusion of the broadcast that night, I was given a Polaroid of myself on television. I was standing, a phone to my ear, wearing a black-and-white-checkered suit, credits rolling over me. Then the stock market crashed on Black Monday and shortly afterward, I was laid off.

My political science major, unfortunately, hasn't set me up for a well-paying job with lots of growth potential. The next step is often graduate school or law school, but I don't want to consider those. I'm not ready to give up on writing. Not yet, anyway.

Both my sisters, one older and one younger, still live at home, and the place feels like a halfway house for women who lack the ability to emotionally regulate. Instead, we all just scream at one another. "You used up all the hot water!" or "Who ate the last banana?!" and "Get out of the bathroom!" My mother, exhausted from spending all day, every day, on her feet serving up cheese samples—she's an assistant manager at Swiss Colony, a cheese and sausage shop in a nearby shopping mall—shouts, "Stop yelling!"

I make my way to Adam Personnel. The receptionist lets me wait there for a moment, and then looks up. "You're here for . . . ?" she asks. "I have an appointment at ten with Peter," I say, the name on the ad I circled in *The New York Times*.

When he comes out to the tiny reception area filled with other job seekers, I'm surprised at how young he is. "Hello," Peter says, shaking my hand and smiling, which causes his moustache to wiggle. There's something odd about the right corner of his mouth, which I will later learn was surgically reconstructed after he bit through an electrical cord as a toddler.

"So you're a writer? Really?" he asks, walking me back to his black metal desk, one of a dozen or so in a large, noisy room.

"Well, I'm a writer, but, I'm, well . . . I'm not really writing now. I'm trying to find a job that will let me write," I say. I have few clips to show for myself—a couple of pieces in the college newspaper and several summaries of NBC Radio shows I wrote as a summer intern.

"I've got a few things that might involve some writing, but we don't get many actual writing jobs," Peter says. "I'm sorry."

He starts asking me what I like to write and that leads to a discussion of my desire to write about music, which leads us to talking about bands we both like.

This guy is so sweet, I think. I wish I were feeling even an ounce of chemistry, but it's not there, although we are having an awfully long interview; in fact we're not even talking job prospects, we're just getting to know each other. Peter tells me he isn't sure what he wants to do with his life (being an employment counselor is just a stop on this unknown journey) other than play bass in a band that he and some friends are starting. He lives rent-free in a house in New Canaan, an affluent Connecticut suburb, where he is the resident tutor and guardian of a bunch of low-income minority boys participating in a program that lets them attend New Canaan's posh public high school. He helps them with their homework, gives them guidance-counselor-type advice, and makes sure they don't break any rules (or if they do, that they break them discreetly).

Our small talk tapers off. I'm here, after all, to find a job. Peter turns to a stack of papers on his desk. "I've got a couple of things you might like," he says, flipping through the pages. "There's a job at the Junior League. Administrative but with a lot of responsibility," he says. I'm not sure if he's joking. The *Junior League*? What is that? Sounds like the Girl Scouts. I shrug. "Okay," I say. "I need a job."

"I'll be in touch then, probably later today or tomorrow," he says. I smile.

"That would be great, thanks so much." I stand to go. "It was really nice talking to you." We shake hands and I head toward the elevator. A few months later Peter will tell me that the moment I left the room, he stood up and shouted, "That's the woman I'm going to marry!" and everyone told him to shut up; some threw rolled-up balls of paper at him.

The elevator door opens, and as I step inside I hear someone else running to catch it, so I hold it open. It's Peter, out of breath, clutching his suit jacket. "Hey," he says, squeezing in as the doors close. "Would you like to have lunch?"

I am dumbstruck. I hardly even know this guy, I'm not going to have lunch with him. But before I can answer he adds, "It's my birthday today."

Right, I think. It's his birthday. "Really?" I say.

"Yeah, really. I'm twenty-three."

"I'm twenty-three too," I say.

"I know," Peter says. "You put your birthdate on your application."

We stare at the descending floor numbers. "I can't, I'm sorry. I already have plans to meet a friend at Hunter College." I remember that Hunter College was a stop on the subway I took to get here.

"Oh, no problem," Peter says, smiling. "Maybe next time." I exit the elevator with such urgency, it's as if this lunch appointment is the most pressing of my life.

The following week I interview with the Junior League. It's a secretarial job. In fact, all the interviews Peter arranges for me are jobs with titles that are euphemisms for *secretary*. Typing fast is apparently my most marketable skill, so I'm ready to just bite the bullet and take whatever is offered to me next. Then Peter calls to tell me he's leaving Adam Personnel and has a career plan of his own. He is moving home, to upstate New York, in preparation for graduate school. He had decided to get a master's degree in chemistry. Peter also tells me that a friend of his from college called to say the law firm where she works is looking to hire legal assistants. She asked if he was interested. "I'm not," Peter told her, "but I have a friend that might be." That friend is me. I interview and get the job, deciding to give it a try. Who knows? I think. Maybe I will love it and really want to go to law school.

A few weeks later Peter leaves New York City and enrolls at the state university in some prerequisite courses he needs in order to apply to graduate programs. "Why chemistry?" I ask.

"I like chemistry," he says, matter-of-fact. "Chemistry is life."

Over the next two years Peter and I are in touch regularly, and we get to know a lot about each other's lives. I learn he was adopted as a baby and that his parents are evangelical Christians. His first philosophy of science course at Cornell made him question everything he believed about the way the world worked; since then he's been a devout atheist, a shift that deeply wounded his parents. Peter's father, a white man and a pastor, leads a largely African American congregation at a local church. His parents' inner city neighborhood is poor and the crack epidemic has hit hard. Addicts often knock on their front door looking for money or food, Peter says, and his mother and father always open it.

"They are good people, but they also take the Bible literally. I mean l-i-t-e-r-a-l-l-y," he says, stretching out the word to magnify its meaning. "Like the earth was 'created' in a week. One week. They really believe that."

Much later, when we are well into our relationship, I will learn that Peter lived in foster care for about four months before being adopted. His mother will tell me that he hadn't been held much as a baby because there were several other young children in that home. The lack of early bonding with a parent likely has something to do with why Peter often feels ill at ease socially. He will tell me that as a kid, he never felt he really fit into—or could truly navigate—the social landscape. The psychologist Erik Erikson, known both for his theory of psychosocial development and the concept of an "identity crisis," said that those who learn to trust caregivers in infancy are more likely to form trusting relationships with others throughout their lives.

Decades later, when I am familiar with Peter's insatiable need for affirmation and acceptance, for validation and gratitude, I will wonder if his adoption had anything to do with this struggle to define and believe in himself. We develop our individual identities in adolescence, and that is much more complicated for someone who has been adopted because of the issues it raises—for instance, the reason a child was given up in the first place. And being adopted is not an attribute in the same way something like gender or ethnicity is. It doesn't help the adoptee figure out their identity; in fact, it makes it more difficult. A number of studies have found that adoptees score lower on measures of self-esteem and self-confidence; a U.S. government report on the impacts of adoption suggested one reason could be that "adopted persons may view themselves as different, out-of-place, unwelcome, or rejected."

I find my job as legal assistant at the firm in the World Trade Center boring. I'm working with lawyers in the tax department, in an area of the law that deals almost exclusively with retirement plans. I have the Internal Revenue Code on my bookshelf, a series of thick books with pages thin as tissue paper, full of byzantine rules and regulations. The language is so obtuse it seems expressly created to perpetuate the need for tax lawyers.

On Friday evenings when the senior partner in the large office across the hall leaves to catch the early train home, a few of us grab leftover cans of soda from the conference room and sit on the velvety couches in his office watching the sun set over the financial district. The waters of New York Harbor sparkle in the orange light, intensified by its reflection off the glass facades of surrounding skyscrapers. The Statue of Liberty looks so small it doesn't seem real; even the cruise ships in the harbor look like toys. With a view like this, I think, it wouldn't be hard to imagine you own the world.

I am part of a large group of legal assistants about my age at the firm, so there is plenty of collegial socializing. We all seem to be using these jobs as way stations between our lives now and whatever comes next, be it graduate school, marriage, or something we haven't yet figured out. I alternate between being so busy I'm driven home in a corporate sedan at two in the morning, and days where I struggle to find something to do. The quiet days I write short stories, look for editorial jobs, and fill pages of yellow legal pads with letters to Peter. We've become good friends and talk on the phone every few weeks about work, school, the dates we've had, books we've read.

Peter keeps inviting me to Ithaca, where he is living with a few other guys, all of them in a band together. He has started graduate school for chemistry at SUNY Binghamton. I know he's interested in me in ways that I'm not interested in him, so I keep making excuses. A year and a half into my stint as a legal assistant, I quit and move to Philadelphia for an editor's job at *Scan,* a small arts magazine that is barely afloat and will likely fold. Still,

I tell myself, it's writing, at least for a while. And that summer, I finally run out of excuses not to visit Peter, so I drive up to Ithaca to see his band, LD50, play at a party.

The house where he lives is in Danby, a small town just south of Ithaca, on a big piece of land with a spectacular view of Cayuga Lake's deep blue water. The band has set up in the garage with the door open, instruments and speakers and tangled wires half inside and half out. Guns N' Roses is blasting through outdoor speakers and although it's only five P.M., everyone seems to be drunk, stoned, or tripping. Peter is a bit toasted himself, as he's been drinking all day and doing lines of coke. I'm uncomfortable at first, mostly because everyone has been partying for hours and I am stone cold sober. I don't do coke or drop acid or even like smoking pot very much, so I'm used to feeling like an outsider when it comes to people around me getting high.

I grab a beer and sit on the grass. As soon as the band starts to play and I see Peter on bass, with his long, curly hair and all his friends around, something changes for me. I never thought of him as boyfriend material, but now, I think, well . . . maybe. After the first set he makes his way over to me and asks what I thought of the music. "You guys sounded great," I say. He takes my hand and introduces me to his bandmates (one of whom is also his housemate). We both know I will have to spend the night, as it's a four-hour drive back to Philly. Peter's room is small, a curtain separating the desk area from his twin bed, which is tucked beneath some wood shelving filled with books and record albums. He has draped a red bandana over the bedside lamp to diffuse and soften the light. That night we do, finally, sleep together, but it's mostly awkward, because we hadn't even kissed yet and suddenly we are having sex. And because Peter has done an awful lot of blow.

The next morning, as I leave to drive back to Philly, our goodbye feels different than usual. "Maybe I can come down to you next weekend and you can show me Philly?" Peter says, leaning into the driver's window of my battered '74 Chevy Nova.

Do I give this another shot? I wonder.

"Yeah, sure. I had a good time," I say, and give his forearm a squeeze. Peter leans in to kiss me. "Me too. I'll call you this week."

The next weekend he drives his red Chevette to my apartment in Philadelphia, and we go see the new Bruce Weber documentary *Let's Get Lost*, about the jazz musician Chet Baker. We spend most of the rest of the weekend in bed, talking, eating ice cream out of the container, and having sex—intimate, tender, non-cocaine-addled sex. And that, as they say, is that. It has taken two years for me to see Peter as more than a friend, but when I finally fall for him, I fall hard. Being around him makes me feel steady inside, grounded. I love his dewy, almond-shaped eyes, his long, curly hair, his strong arms and soothing voice. I love that he knows the world in a way I don't, knows it physically and understands the mechanics and processes underlying it. I can spend hours telling him stories about the people I work with, my writing, books I've read, my family, and he never loses interest. He doesn't laugh often, but when he does it's wonderful—a big spreading smile, a deep satisfying laugh. I love that when we lie in bed together at night, he will put the perfect album on the turntable, old Isley Brothers or Chick Corea.

In August, I leave my job in Philadelphia to be an editorial assistant at *Glamour* magazine in New York City, and that fall, I travel upstate to meet Peter's family for the first time. I am there for Thanksgiving dinner. Before the meal begins, we join hands and his father thanks Lord Jesus for our health and well-being, for the food before us, and then asks him to have mercy on homosexuals, currently being punished by the deadly AIDS virus. With bowed head, I look sideways at Peter, who just squeezes my hand.

We leave the next morning after a brief visit to the church, arriving late enough to see only his father's sermon (much to the chagrin of Peter's mother). After the service, an army of older women—grandmothers and great-grandmothers—come up to Peter and tenderly touch his hands, hold his face, or hug him. He grew up in front of them, in this church, and they adore him. He bends down a little to let each of them hug him, and he speaks loudly, leaning into their ears. His hair is gathered into a ponytail that hangs down his back and he's wearing the only collared shirt he owns.

Being three hours' drive apart is hard for both of us, and I feel like I'm spending my weeks waiting for the weekend, when we can see each other. On Valentine's Day, Peter drives to New York City with a dozen long-stemmed red roses he can't afford and surprises me at *Glamour*'s offices. Some of the girls I work with are peeking into the reception area and giggling. Betty, the receptionist, calls me and says, "Your boyfriend is here. He's cute!" And there he is, standing in the reception area with his big bouquet, sincere and sweet and a little embarrassed, unsure how to handle all the attention he's getting.

A few months later I quit my job at the magazine—I've been there barely a year—and move in with Peter. He is still in graduate school, and I am tired of answering phones for editors. Peter and I live in a two-room cottage in tiny Marathon, New York, with dairy farmers for neighbors. He spends a lot of his time in Binghamton, about thirty minutes' drive south, in the university's chemistry lab finishing the research for his master's thesis. I have a thirty-minute commute to the small city of Cortland, where I am now a reporter for the *Cortland Standard* newspaper, earning $6.25 an hour. It's the kind of small-town newspaper where finished stories are sent via pneumatic tubes across the floor and down two flights to the folks in layout. My beats are education (there is a branch of the state university here) and dairy farming, and my editor's name is Skip. Working there is like being in a movie about a small-town newspaper, one in which I have an important role, the beat reporter. And that feels good.

Although it's a big adjustment, it's also springtime in upstate New York and surreally beautiful. My drive to work at sunrise is breathtaking, the sky pinking up as I head north. All around me are undulating green hillsides dotted with clusters of cows nibbling on grass and alfalfa, fields of wild daisies, brown-eyed Susans, yellow honeysuckle, and dense bushes of white aster and milkweed.

A few weeks into my new reporting job, while interviewing a local farmer about his expansion plans, I get the chance to milk a cow for the first time. The farmer gives me a pair of too-big rubber boots in which to wade through barn muck, and then sits me down on an upside-down metal bucket—just as I imagined he would—and shows me how to hold the cow's udder. The trick to getting the milk to come out, he tells me, is to pull somewhere between too gently and too hard.

Seven months later it's November, and the dark and cold are starting to get to me. I'm feeling low and missing New York City, thinking maybe I made a mistake leaving my job at *Glamour*. Maybe if I had just stuck it out, I would have moved beyond the world of editorial assistants and it would have gotten better. Since Peter and I moved into this little cottage in Marathon something has changed in our relationship, something subtle but significant, and I'm not sure what it is. All I know is I'm alone an awful lot, and Peter spends more and more time in his lab at school in Binghamton.

I get home from my newspaper job around three-thirty in the afternoon, because the paper comes out at one P.M. and my day starts at six-fifteen in the morning. Often Peter doesn't get home until eight or nine in the evening. I'm no longer sure why I rushed to be here with him, since I barely see him. Then again, I do know. I was afraid our relationship wouldn't last, that whatever it was about me Peter had fallen for wouldn't be enough to keep his long-distance interest. I was insecure and anxious and didn't like our being apart, didn't find the phone an adequate substitute for the flesh-and-blood man. But now, when we are together, Peter is so exhausted he's sleeping most of the time. We had more intimacy when we were 300 miles apart, I keep thinking. I'm lonely. I have developed an irrational crush on a very attractive and very married city official and I'm often stuck in my own head, lamenting how far I've come, from a job in the Manhattan high-rise offices of a national magazine to writing about dairy parades and zoning board meetings.

When I get like this, I remind myself that I am, finally, writing for a living, interesting small-town stories like the one about a cult-like church trying to proselytize the town's teens, and some very passionate opposition to a proposal to bury low-level radioactive waste near here. And even though Peter works a lot, we do find time to have fun in between the demands of graduate school and newspaper reporting.

In late spring he invites some of the students from his lab over for a potluck dinner. Most of them are Polish and Russian, and it turns into a raucous Eastern European–themed party with plenty of vodka and kielbasa and someone's Shostakovich album on the turntable. In June we go to the Cortland County Dairy Parade and watch the newly crowned Dairy Princess wave to us from atop her float. It is a warm day, and after the parade and lunch we drive to Buttermilk Falls State Park in Ithaca and hike a few of the trails, water tumbling down the rocks beside us. In August we visit Peter's grandparents in the tiny town of Bellefontaine, Ohio, about an hour northwest of Columbus. On the drive there, the starter in

Peter's Chevette dies, so we can't turn off the engine until we reach his grandparents' house. Peter and his grandfather, Melrose, who is in his eighties, go to the auto parts store in town and then work together, slowly, to take apart the insides of the car and replace its starter. Peter is relaxed and patient with his grandfather, clearly enjoying the discussion of cables to be disconnected, the bolts, brackets, and battery that need to be removed in order to get to the car's broken starter. I can hear the two of them chatting about other things too, graduate school, me, Peter's parents.

While they work on the car, his grandmother Grace takes me on a tour of the senior center, where she and her husband are active members, and she introduces me to every person there. Then it is off to the market, where we buy some things for dinner. She is like a storybook grandmother, gentle and sweet, always smiling and saying things like "Well now, let's sit here and visit for a while." My own maternal grandmother couldn't be more different. She came to New York City in the 1920s, a Jewish refugee fleeing Russian pogroms in Poland. She is serious, speaks in heavily accented English, and throws salt superstitiously over her shoulder. Grace and Melrose tool around town on a bicycle built for two and Grace cooks things like chicken and biscuits and puts green Jell-O in her salads. My grandmother has never owned a bicycle; she feeds us kosher brisket and matzoh ball soup.

After dinner, Peter's grandparents take out photo albums and show me photos of Peter as a little boy, an orange life jacket around his shoulders, fishing with his grandfather and proudly holding up his catch, which is dripping wet and still connected to the hook at the end of the line.

It snowed last week, the first week of November, the farms and hillsides around us covered in a white so bright that even when it's not sunny, I have to shield my eyes or they burn and tear. Now and then we spend the evening with another couple, both of them also graduate students in the chemistry department. The four of us go to dive bars deep in the country, the kind that still have jukeboxes with music from the 1950s and large wooden shuffleboard tables. On Sundays, the one morning Peter and I usually sleep in, he runs downstairs in his sweatpants to start a fire in the wood-burning stove and then races back up to me, jumping into the bed with a howl from the cold. We burrow under the covers to keep warm, talking and laughing until the cottage heats up.

Two months later, in January, Peter finishes his master's thesis. I'm thanked in the acknowledgments for both my typing skills and my patience, and soon we'll be moving. Peter has a job offer from Cytogen, an early-stage pharmaceutical company in Princeton, New Jersey. I start calling everyone I know in New Jersey to try and wrangle a job at a newspaper, trade magazine, nonprofit, anywhere that will let me write. The only thing I find is a job in Baltimore as features editor at the alternative weekly there, the *City Paper*. Midmonth, Peter leaves Binghamton to start his job, staying with friends of mine while searching for a place we can live, somewhere between Princeton and Baltimore.

I am on my own in the cottage now, for what I assumed would be a tedious month of work and sitting at home. The big activity of the evenings would be starting a fire in the wood-burning stove without my hair catching fire (which has happened twice), then reading and bed. It is nothing like that. It is surprisingly wonderful. I finally do some good reporting because I stop looking at everything here as inconsequential small potatoes and begin to appreciate my role in the fabric of the community. Everyone reads the paper in Cortland and that means everyone knows my name. They call me during the day with news tips and comments on my stories. I start socializing a little with some of the single reporters. Turns out that one of my colleagues, Jackie, another female reporter, is in a relationship with a woman, but in this neck of the woods that information is mostly kept private.

She and her girlfriend, Natalie, rent a small house on a street I've never seen before. Inside it's wood floors and jute rugs with geometric designs and hand-me-down furniture, same as I have. We have dinner and wine, and they talk about leaving Cortland so they can come out and be a couple in public. We gossip about the paper and its editors. "I wish you weren't leaving," Jackie says. "Just when we're getting to know you better." There's a part of me wishing I wasn't leaving too. I've been so much happier the last few weeks with Peter gone, although I miss him. It's like there are two people inside me, one who misses him and one who wants him to go live his life while I stay in the cottage, keep working at the paper, make new friends, and build my own separate life. The thought of joining Peter, as I will do in a couple of weeks, feels like a relief—we're out of this freezing place!—but also a new beginning I know on some level I haven't exactly chosen.

By February I've left Marathon and the newspaper for Philadelphia, where we will live and from where I will commute to Baltimore by train. We've conscripted as many of our friends as we can to help us move into a loft on the corner of Ninth and Arch Street, a stone's throw from a big mall and around the corner from the Trocadero, a music club. The loft is roomy, precisely because it has no rooms—it is the top floor of a brick building. It's also cheap—$500 a month—located three floors above a Chinese restaurant.

Moving weekend, we pack up what little we have in the cottage, get the rest of our belongings out of storage, and drive to Philadelphia. On the way, we stop at my father's house in Hackettstown, New Jersey, near the Delaware Water Gap. We are here to pick up an old couch, a love seat, and a large area rug he and his girlfriend no longer need. "What are you going to do with this?" my dad asks, motioning toward the couch—which has seen better days—with his chin, his hands in his pockets. "It's got a few holes in it." The three of us are standing in a big storage building that houses an old car, some furniture, and a ferocious German shepherd named Max. My dad and Carol bought this house on ten acres—complete with a little pond—when they left New York City, about four years ago.

Carol seems like a fish out of water so far from Manhattan. She has thrown all her energy into decorating the house, which looks like the outcome of a duel between *Country Living* magazine and Bloomingdale's.

"You could cover it with something, like—" She coughs and covers her mouth with the back of her hand, the nails polished deep red. "Like a drop cloth," she says, taking a drag of her cigarette. "You just go to a paint store and ask for a white drop cloth, you know? Those heavy cloths for catching paint splatter, but you could drape them over the couches and just staple them underneath."

"Burt," she says, turning toward my father, who is talking to Peter. "Do we have a staple gun we can lend them?" Carol turns to me. "It'll be like a quick reupholstery job."

By the time we get to the apartment building in Philly, our friends are already outside, waiting for us. We grab furniture and boxes out of the U-Haul and drag them up three flights of stairs. It's an unusually warm spring day, and the breeze holds a glimpse of summer in it. After all our junk is upstairs, we sit inside the empty truck, the door still rolled up, and drink cans of cold beer.

It's the hottest summer of our lives. The loft—we can't afford an air conditioner—is like a brick oven. At night, Peter and I drive around in our 4Runner with its air-conditioning on high, away from downtown to the neighborhood of Manayunk, where we get soft ice cream, perch on the hood of the car, and try to feel a breeze off the river. Three years ago, I was working right around the corner from here in the offices of that tiny arts magazine, *Scan* (which went belly-up nine months after I came on board). I was dating Peter then but not exclusively, feeling free and happy, getting paid to write. Now I'm sitting on the hood of a car that belongs to my boyfriend, the engine making ticking sounds as it tries to cool in the ninety-degree heat. Why is it I felt more confident back then, more important to Peter? I wonder. I glance at him lazily licking his ice cream cone. Maybe for him it's the difference between chasing what you want and getting it.

The sun is setting over the Schuylkill River and my mind is back at *Scan* and how proud I felt every day walking in there, even though most of us knew very little about publishing a magazine. Now I travel two and a half hours a day, each way, to Baltimore for a job as a features editor at a weekly newspaper, which I got thanks to a friend on the staff. I have come to understand that I don't know the first thing about editing someone else's work— I only know how to write. I am anxious and insecure, exhausted by the five-hour daily commute. I know in my heart it can't last, but for this moment at least, I am employed and the breeze feels good. I have held on to Peter, moved with him and for him, and found a job in journalism. I am twenty-six years old and committed to this man, not sure I'd find another person I could love this much, with whom I could talk about so many things, someone this intelligent, who lets me tell him the plots of all the novels I read, whose very heartbeat makes me feel at peace. We're together, I think. This is working.

Ten months later, Peter and I decide to get married. It's February and we are talking about his birthday in two months. I ask him what he wants. "Why don't we get married?" he says. "I have three pay periods in March. So that's like an extra paycheck. Why don't we get married, and then you will have health insurance?" The *City Paper* can't afford to provide health insurance to its employees. It's something I'm worried about and we've talked about, but haven't found any good solutions other than for me to find another job. Getting married solves that problem, it's true, although this is the least romantic marriage proposal I can imagine.

On the other hand, I wasn't expecting a down-on-one-knee kind of thing, Peter offering up a black-velvet ring box. I don't see myself as the kind of woman who receives a diamond ring or has a wedding that requires debates about caterers and color schemes. Other women might be the star of that kind of fairy tale, but not me. I have convinced myself—perhaps because I know this is what Peter wants to believe about me—that I am completely nontraditional, just as Peter feels is true about himself. So why on earth would I want a traditional marriage proposal? Or wedding? Looking back, I suppose I was afraid to admit to Peter that deep down, I *did* want that—or at least some of that. A few weeks from now, when we tell my mom we're getting married, she will be so excited that she'll dig out her wedding gown, tucked in a silver box in a bedroom closet. She will tell me to try it on and see if it fits. And I will. My mother had it custom-made and it's stunning and simple, white taffeta with a pearl-studded neckline. It is so tiny, I will barely get it zipped up. When I show myself to Peter, twirling once, he will laugh. "You look like the Good Witch of the North," he'll tell me. Yeah, I'll agree, embarrassed for thinking this was an option, acting as if I'm in on the joke.

Later on, in midlife, I will better understand why it was so hard for me to ask for what I wanted back then, to admit that I actually loved that dress and wanted to wear it. Lots of things conspire to create or cut down someone's sense of their own worth. In my life it wasn't one big thing but many, many small ones, a collection of insults and humiliations that piled up over time until they were bigger than I was. And the piling up started early.

As a kid, my teeth were so badly misaligned I wore heavy silver braces for four years. I went through puberty late because I was underweight, which left me underdeveloped compared to my curvaceous classmates. My father told me many times, "It's a good thing you're smart, because you're not pretty." It created an odd juxtaposition of feelings in me, believing my father loved me while he also humiliated me, like when he called me "Stupe"—shorthand for *stupid*—because I struggled with my math homework. Or asked me when the hell I was going to get my period. Or when he threatened to send me to "the skinny kids farm" if I didn't start eating more. I often begged him in tears not to send me away, believing I was about to be packed up and sent to Mr. Brown, the name of the fake head of this nonexistent punishment camp for society's underweight children. He and my mother stopped short of packing my bags but instead made me sit at our dining room table in the dark for hours, in front of a cold plate of unfinished pot roast or meat loaf. I would lay my head down on the table and daydream that I was someplace else. Hours later, my mother, silently siding with my father, would scrape the uneaten food on my plate into the kitchen trash can and, without looking at me, tell me to go to bed.

In school I felt like an ugly outsider, Jewish in a community of largely Irish and Italian Catholic kids, ashamed that my family was different, that we celebrated different holidays and ate different food. In seventh grade, someone painted the word *Jew* in red across my locker.

By the time I got to high school, my parents were so involved with their own disintegrating marriage they knew little about my life. They didn't even know if I had applied to college, although my father eventually asked. When I said I had, he made sure I understood that he wouldn't be able to pay for it, and my mother didn't have any savings of her own. "You can't get blood from a stone," my father often said, any time he feared I might be thinking about asking him for some financial help. The small amount of money my parents had put aside for college—about $900— they gave to my older sister, who dropped out before the end of her first year.

That is how I become the kind of woman who gets married because she needs health insurance, who does not expect a romantic marriage proposal, who gets married because she's afraid if she doesn't, the man she loves will change his mind and then no one will want her.

The truth is, at least on some level, I hate the thought of being someone's wife. Marriage turned my mother from a vivacious, interesting, happy woman—one I know about from stories and old photos—into a depressed and lonely wife. My father was rarely home when I was growing up, and the enduring image I have of my mom is her standing at the kitchen sink, hands encased in yellow rubber gloves, doing dishes after dinner. Sometimes she would just stand at the sink holding a sudsy plate for several minutes, staring blankly out the kitchen window into the backyard. Most nights my father wasn't home. He moonlighted as a driver for Air Brook Limousine, both because we needed the extra money and because it gave him the cover and freedom to have lengthy affairs with other women. My mom waited at home for something to change, and my dad led a double life.

"Okay," I say. "Let's get married."

Peter laughs. "That was easy."

Only one condition, he tells me. He doesn't want to do any of the planning. "I can't deal with that," he says. "Also I'm really busy at work." Peter is a bench chemist (*bench* being chemist shorthand for a lab table) at Cytogen, which is a lot like being a line cook in a restaurant kitchen. The Ph.D.s are the chefs, creating recipes for compounds they want to test, and the bench chemists mix up the ingredients. He is adamant about preventing our families from getting involved in the planning. "Just find a place and we can do it in the next two months. Let's keep our mothers out of it," he says. "Let's do it our way."

"Our way" of course, is really his way, I realize, with me doing all the work. Two months to plan and execute a wedding on a small budget. Peter has removed himself from the entire process, although he's paying for it. Yet that's okay with me. I'm invested in this relationship and this man; I hope getting married will pave the way for stability, a family, a more mature love.

A few nights later we are in New Jersey visiting my dad and we decide to go out for pizza and tell him we're getting married. "We have something to tell you," I say, when the three of us are seated. My father starts smiling. He already knows, I think. He's probably dreamed of this moment. He desperately wants each of his daughters married, wants someone else to be taking care of them, even though he has done little caretaking himself. He told us years ago that he had $5,000 saved for each of us, which we could have when we got married. A carrot, he hoped, would motivate each of us to get the job done. At my older sister's wedding a few years earlier, he seemed downright giddy to be checking her off his list, despite the fact that his $90 monthly child support payments to my mother—so small they were more symbolic than anything else—ended long ago.

"We're getting married," I say. My father's smile is two feet wide. "That's fantastic, congratulations!" He stands up to hug me and then hugs Peter. "When?" he asks, and we all sit down again. "Probably April, in Philly. Eilene is planning it." Yes, we acknowledge, it's quick, and no, I'm not pregnant. Quick is how we want it, and so that's how we're doing it. "Especially," Peter adds, "since we're paying for it."

My father nods approvingly. This is language he understands: the language of money and control. If Peter and I are paying for our wedding, we don't have to explain the timing. Money is something my father covets and respects, although he has never had much of it. And like my father, who can tell you every single dime he's ever spent on you, Peter also keeps score when it comes to money. He points out the things for which he has paid almost like he's flexing a muscle. There's the wok we bought last week, the white paint we're going to use this weekend to spruce up the loft, the take-out Chinese food we had on Thursday night, the car payments. I'm hoping that after we're married this kind of claim-staking will become unnecessary, a vestige of our prenuptial past.

Peter excuses himself to use the bathroom and my dad stares at his hands on the wooden table, one folded on top of the other, and then turns to look at me. "Don't blow it," he says, his smile gone. I can feel my face getting hot. There are a million things I want to say in response, but I'm so shocked I can't form sentences, other than to say "I won't." I am burning with shame and embarrassment. I wish I had been indignant instead, had stood up angrily and shot back, "Why aren't you saying this to Peter?" Why didn't my father think I was special, that I was the great catch here? At that moment, though, his words felt like the truth, an obvious one that didn't need to be stated. *Of course* I wouldn't blow it. Did my father think I was an idiot? That I didn't understand how undeservedly lucky I was that this smart, handsome, ambitious, sweet man I'd fallen in love with had also fallen for me?

What I didn't understand then was that my "falling" for Peter likely had as much to do with my father as it did with Peter. Research has found that whether or not a father is absent or present, emotionally available or emotionally distant, critical, supportive or indifferent, has a significant effect on the type of man his daughter chooses as a husband, and her interactions with him. It also affects a daughter's self-image and self-esteem. Linda Nielsen, a professor of adolescent and educational psychology at Wake Forest University who has studied father-daughter relationships since the 1970s, says a present, involved, supportive father builds up his daughter's self-confidence and passes along the implicit message that she does not need a man to make her valuable. "If a young woman gets that affirmation and approval from her dad, she is not going to be desperate to get it anywhere else because she already has it in him," Nielsen said in a 2015 interview. This was not the message I got from my father. The message I got was "Don't blow it."

Peter comes back to the table. My father is smiling again and just like that, we pick up the conversation where we left off.

I decide we'll get married at the Warwick Hotel in downtown Philadelphia. For the reception, our guests will commandeer the hotel's Sunday brunch, which takes place in a bright, open area in the hotel's historic lobby. I reserve a small banquet room for the brief ceremony. There will be chairs, lots of standing room, and champagne. And Peter's father will marry us.

On the phone, Peter explains to him that my Jewish relatives aren't comfortable with the word *Jesus*. "You can use the word *God*, you just can't use the word *Jesus*, okay? So *no Jesus*. God is fine. As much God as you want. Okay Pops? But no Jesus." As long as the reverend can invoke the name of the Lord in some way, he's good with it.

On my lunch hour in Baltimore, I duck into a store that sells Crane's stationery and buy fancy cards with a border of blue flowers on which I handwrite invitations to fifty-one people. I order a chocolate wedding cake (I figure if we're going to do it "our way," I want an all-chocolate cake).

The day of our wedding, we're up early. Some of our friends will come back to the loft after brunch, for drinks and snacks. I've stocked up on beer, wine, vodka, mixers, and Maker's Mark bourbon, a favorite of Peter's pals from Ithaca. That morning, after his shower, he walks out of the bathroom with a towel around his waist and shaving cream on his face. Holding the razor in his hand, he says suddenly, "Right now all these people we know are getting up and getting dressed and preparing to come here to Philly, just for us." It's the closest to beaming I've ever seen him. "Yeah," I say. "It is kind of cool." Peter leaves the house first, taking a cab, as I am coming a bit later and driving myself. It's our one nod to tradition—the bride walking in last.

My wedding dress, which is not actually a wedding dress, is a gift from Carol. It's a cocktail-length, cream-colored linen dress with a macramé top, long sleeves, and shoulder pads. I bought it, alone, at a Lord & Taylor department store in New Jersey. Carol gave me the money for the dress but didn't actually go shopping with me; neither did my mother. A couple of weeks later, I take the dress to my mom's apartment, to model it for her. When I express my hatred for the shoulder pads and a determination to remove them, my mother says, "No, no, leave them in! Without those pads," she sighs, "you'll look like there's nothing to you."

I keep them in and hate that the white pads look like gauze bandages under the shoulders of the macramé sleeves. For years, I will look at my wedding photos and wish I had done what I wanted and snipped the pads out, but at that point in my life, and for decades afterward, I wasn't confident enough to follow my own intuition. I was always asking other people what I should do and giving their thoughts and feelings far more weight than my own. If things went wrong, it wasn't my fault, and if they went right, it only proved that I should trust other people's instincts before my own.

My entrance at the hotel, into the room where I will be married, is unceremonious. I am uncomfortable being the center of attention, so I start talking to whoever is in front of me, taking photos with them, and then find my way over to my grandmother and mother. Peter is making the rounds too. His hair is at a difficult length—he cut it as he neared the end of graduate school and was interviewing for jobs but after he was hired as a chemist, decided to grow it long again—and this middle stage is a little incoherent. He is wearing a black leather jacket and a tie we chose together, the tie being the most expensive piece of clothing he has ever owned, $60, hand-painted with blue and green flowers. My mother takes one look at him and whispers to me, "Why isn't he wearing a suit?"

"He didn't want to," I say. She just stares at me.

"He's wearing a tie," I offer. My mother wrinkles her nose and shakes her head as if there is a nasty smell in the room. "He has no respect for you," she says. "I'm very disappointed in him."

The ceremony hasn't even started yet and my mother is already disappointed. "Mom, please, can you just let it go? I'm about to get married. This is who he is, it's fine. It's a jacket. Who cares?'

"Do *you* care?" she asks.

I shrug my padded shoulders. Yes, I care. I care a great deal, actually. I tried to convince Peter to wear a sports jacket and tie—forget about a suit but at least a proper jacket. And he pushed back, hard. He was not about to let "all that traditional wedding bullshit" force him to wear something he didn't want to wear and would never wear again (or so he thought). He wanted to be the guy that got married in a leather jacket and flowered tie, and I didn't want to have a showdown over it. But underneath, I agree, just a little, with my mother. I wanted to be marrying a man who would wear a suit to his wedding, but that man is not Peter. Instead I asked myself, "Do you want to risk a huge argument and potentially having to call off the wedding because you don't agree with Peter's fashion tastes? Because you want him to wear a suit to his wedding, something he finds repugnant and ordinary?" Of course not.

I leave my mother (silently fuming over the leather jacket) and find Peter, in a corner laughing with my girlfriends. He is shy and they are easy for him, chatty and funny. I walk over and whisper that we need to get started. A hotel employee stands guard over a corner table covered in fluted glasses. I begin moving toward the front of the room and see my old college friend John and his wife, Dina. He is holding their four-month-old daughter, so small and adorable she looks like a toy. I hadn't seen them come in, so I hug them. "Congratulations," Dina says, smiling.

"Thank you," I say, and I can feel my eyes starting to tear up. The anxiety I've been feeling all morning is beginning to overtake me. When I was alone in our loft getting ready, after Peter had left for the hotel, I told myself it was completely natural to have some pre-wedding jitters. My married friends were all a bit of a wreck before their ceremonies; one good friend was on Xanax the whole time. But why, I wonder, if we all claim to want this, are we so panicked beforehand?

And now, with Dina, my doubt is bubbling up again, threatening my composure. I'm starting to look for the exit, a panic attack barely at bay. Dina asks, "Are you okay?"

Peter is waiting at the front of the room, talking to his sister, his father looking over his notes, and the roar of conversation is dulling. "It's just . . ." I say, and I am afraid I might cry. "Do you think I'm making a mistake?" I blurt out. "Being married is good, right? I should do this, right?" Dina, still postpartum, her blood coursing with a broth of maternal hormones, is tearing up too. She puts a hand to her chest and says, "Oh god, you're breaking my heart," and wipes at her own eyes. "Yes, yes, of course! Being married is work, but it's good," she says, giving me another hug and looking me in the eye. "It's good."

"Okay," I say, nodding and giving Dina's hand a squeeze. Don't worry about me, the squeeze says. I'm being crazy.

I take a deep breath and exhale slowly, as if I am preparing to jump out of an airplane with a parachute I am not convinced will open. "Okay," I say again, mostly to myself this time. And then I walk to join Peter at the front of the room.

■ TWO

August 2008

IT IS A HOT night in San Diego and Peter and I are lying in bed, staring up at the ceiling fan. It's late and our kids are asleep. Anna, now twelve years old, is in the bedroom next door and her ten-year-old brother Evan is just down the hall. Peter and I have been married for eighteen years. We've got a house in the suburbs and own a minivan and two cars; our children are about to start their first year at private school. My husband isn't a scientist anymore. He left the profession after four years, deciding that he didn't want to be stuck at a lab table breathing in chemicals for the rest of his life. Instead, he headed to law school in New Hampshire and after that, began a new career as an intellectual property attorney at a midsize law firm in San Diego. We had lived in San Diego for two years in the early 1990s, when Peter worked for a pharmaceutical company there, and he had fallen in love with Southern California. At the end of law school he received offers from firms in San Diego and New York City; he chose the sun and surf. It was 1997, we had an eight-month-old daughter, and I figured I could freelance from anywhere. Now, eleven years and four law firms later, Peter is edging into his third year as a partner at the firm Wilson Sonsini Goodrich & Rosati.

Tonight, the plan was supposed to be dinner and a movie. It is our monthly stab at propping up a relationship that seems so steeped in dysfunction it is hard to imagine how food and passive entertainment will make it better. Yet we feel we owe it to each other and, of course, to our children to try. As Peter often reminded me when our daughter was a baby, crying and needy and not sleeping (and as a result I, too, was crying and needy and not sleeping): "She didn't ask to be here. We wanted her." True. And because we had, indeed, wanted both Anna and Evan, we feel an obligation to try and make our marriage better. Hence, these monthly weekend date nights.

Peter, though, isn't in the mood to go out. When we did this last month, he nearly fell asleep during the movie, and when we got home, he went straight to his office in the garage to work. What should have been a night where we reconnected emotionally and physically ended with him in his office and me going to bed. And now here we are, the start of Labor Day weekend, both of us lying in bed and awake at the same time—a rarity. Peter tends to stay up until midnight or later; I am in bed by ten-thirty.

The air-conditioning in the house creates a low insulating hum and feeling of privacy, even though our bedroom shares a wall with Anna's. "Why didn't you want to go out tonight? I thought we were trying to do date night once a month," I say, thinking of the effort it took to get a babysitter. Peter says nothing.

"Is it work?" I ask.

I'm frustrated and angry and hurt. We rarely have a conversation lasting more than ten minutes and now, I'm thinking, he's giving up on monthly dates.

There follows such a long pause that for a second, I think Peter might have fallen asleep. But then, without looking at me, he says, "No, it's not work. It's something else." I feel a stab of panic in my stomach. I say, "What? What is it?" Because I am who I am—part of a long line of anxious Jewish women who always assume the worst, and the worst is usually cancer—I assume something is physically wrong with Peter and he's been afraid to tell me, so my stance softens. "What, Peter? What's wrong?" I ask.

"I have something to tell you," he says.

"Okay," I say. "It's okay, you can tell me."

And then he says it. "I slept with someone else." He's still not looking at me.

At first, I'm not sure I heard right. He slept with someone else? Someone who? We've been together for nearly twenty years and I know—I think—everything about this man, from the sound of his heartbeat to his hatred of raw tomatoes to his favorite authors.

"What?" I say, confused. "You mean, you had sex with someone else?"

"Yes," Peter says. "Three or four times."

"You? You are having an *affair*?" I'm incredulous. This is a man who told me he couldn't be unfaithful because he would feel too guilty and he was a terrible liar. And anyway, women never even gave him a second glance.

"Aren't you?" he asks, turning toward me. "I just assumed you were too."

"No," I say. "I'm not."

My body starts to shake. It starts in my stomach and just

spreads through my body, like tree roots growing in a time-lapse video. It's a cross between shaking and shivering, because suddenly I feel cold, so cold. "Oh my god," Peter says, sitting up. I've rolled over onto my side. "I'm sorry this is making you so upset. Eilene, god . . . look at you. Christ. You said that if things didn't change, you were going to be with other guys."

Not exactly. Once, a few years ago, I told Peter that if we didn't do something to make our relationship better, I could not stay married to him after our kids left for college. I said we needed to spend time together, have sex more than once a month, get into counseling. We were standing halfway inside the hall linen closet, whispering. "Do whatever you need to do," he said, his mouth clenched, eyes closed for a second, as if the sight of me disgusted him. "I'm doing the best I can."

There was a time, not so far in the past, when Peter and I would go to bed at the same time in order to read to each other, usually poetry—e. e. cummings, Elizabeth Bishop, Rilke, Jane Kenyon. During that period in our lives we often drove in the car together for long stretches to get out into the wilderness, like the summer we drove the Alaska Highway for sixteen days, starting in Seattle and ending at the Arctic Circle, where Peter carried me like a new bride over its threshold. "Welcome to the Arctic!" he had said, laughing, and we camped under a midnight sun. Or the time we walked to Tijuana with a co-worker of Peter's to see the band Living Color, feeling daring as we crossed the border into Mexico, partied at the bars on Avenida Revolución, and ate street tacos from a tiny roadside shack. We were enthralled by the lights, sounds, and smells, people hawking Mexican blankets, cheap silver jewelry, and knockoff designer clothes; we gave money to the little kids lining the road back to the border crossing, selling packages of Chiclets.

That night in the linen closet years later, when Peter made me feel like nothing more than a needy nuisance, I wanted to scream, "You used to like me! You wanted to spend fifteen hours a day in the car with me, driving winding roads, walking to Mexico. You wanted to sleep with me. Remember? Do you remember?"

Now I just try to set the record straight. "I said if things didn't change I would leave when Evan went to college." My words are coming out in bursts, between shakes. "I have never been with anyone else." Peter puts his head in his hands. I can't imagine who he's fucking. Or when he does it. Every day he gets home from work and can't even eat dinner until he takes a nap, he's so exhausted.

"Is it someone I know?" I ask. I am facing away from him, my head cradled in the crook of my left arm, and I'm in the throes of a full-blown panic attack, worse than any I've ever had. My body is actually shaking the bed. "No, it's not anyone you know," he says as gently as possible. "Eilene, what can I do to help? What do you want me to do?"

He hugs me from behind, trying to calm me down, but it's like I'm under water. It's two in the morning and pitch-black except for slivers of moonlight that peek through slats in the window blinds. Everything in the house is quiet, our kids deep in sleep, our old bed indented and softened in all the right places, fitted to our bodies after so many years. None of what is happening right now feels real. My husband is having an affair. My marriage is about to end, and I had no idea. But Peter did.

I feel duped, deceived, humiliated. Peter went and got what he needed—love, attention, intimacy—when I did without. Sure, we are miserable, I used to think, but at least we're miserable together.

Marriage has made me feel lonelier and more invisible than I have at any other time in my life. I think I could walk into our kitchen any weekday morning naked wearing an elephant mask and stand right in front of Peter, and he would just ask me to move aside so he could reach the coffee maker. I want, so badly, to have someone look at me as more than just the mother/maid/cook. In my mind, right now, Peter is having an affair with a voluptuous blonde ten years younger than I am with a bikini wax and underwear from the Victoria's Secret window display.

"Eilene," he says again, gingerly. "Do you want me to leave?" I don't want him to leave. I'm scared to death. I'm about to beg him to stay. "No," I say. "No, no. It's okay, I understand. I know you're very unhappy. I am too." And I really do understand. I know he doesn't think I love him, or love him enough. I am certainly not perfect. I have kissed someone else.

I told our marriage counselor about it eighteen months ago, after hastily arranging an "emergency" session. "I made out, for like, two minutes, with a friend last night in a car after an event. What should I do? Should I tell Peter?" Arlene, the therapist, knows my marriage. Peter and I have been in counseling with her for a year. Well, I have been in counseling for a year; Peter makes it about half the time. I arrange our appointments after clearing the date with him and remind him a couple of days before, then the day before, and finally the morning of the appointment. Sometimes Peter calls me as I am pulling into the parking spot by Arlene's office to say he isn't going to make it, that something has come up at the office and he can't get away. Or sometimes I am already sitting in Arlene's office, on her neutral-colored love seat with the tissue box thoughtfully resting within arm's reach, and Peter just doesn't show up.

"Do you love him?" Arlene asked eighteen months ago about the man I kissed in the car. "No, no," I said, laughing. "We're just friends. It's just . . . I am so lonely. But it's not going to happen again." Arlene's advice, essentially, is that sometimes a kiss really is just a kiss. "I think it's fine to just let it go. It happens. You're in couples counseling, you're working on these issues."

But we aren't working on them, I thought then, and now I am angry and resentful and increasingly nasty and dismissive. I have wanted to end my marriage for years, but it feels—and has always felt—impossible. And terrifying. I am almost completely dependent on my husband financially and, at the same time, I'm almost completely responsible for raising our children and maintaining our domestic life. I am a freelance writer and (as much as I despise the word I also know it's true) a *housewife;* Peter is a partner in a law firm. The difference in our salaries is astronomical. How will I survive financially in such an expensive city without him? I don't even know where our money actually *is*, in what bank accounts or in which investments. I have never paid the mortgage. I don't even know *how* to pay a mortgage. I'm a business writer and a feminist, and yet I don't know a thing about our money, which I find shameful and embarrassing. The truth is, I don't even consider it our money. It's Peter's.

All these years as Peter pursued a coveted law partnership, spending most of his time working and sleeping, I was doing the domestic work so many wives do: taking care of the kids, grocery shopping, housecleaning, preparing meals, supervising homework, arranging playdates, and picking up dry cleaning. I trust Peter, so let him focus on money—saving, spending, investing—and I will focus on kids, home, and my freelance work. Only after our divorce will I see how this arrangement—and my own consequent ignorance—hurt me in so many ways, including negotiating my divorce settlement.

At this moment, though, I'm more worried about Anna and Evan than anything else. How will it impact them if we separate? Sure, Peter isn't exactly a model of involved parenting, but he does play an important role in his children's lives. My mind goes back to last summer, when Evan was fascinated by cars and had been building his own collection of them out of Legos. One Saturday morning, he and I decided to try and build a ramp for racing those cars. I was going to cut down the legs of a small table we didn't use and see if I could somehow create a ramp with it. Peter walked out of the garage office to refill his coffee and saw Evan and me hunched over the table, a little saw in my hand. "What's that?" he asked. "What are you doing with the saw?" I told him my plan. He looked at Evan, then back at me.

"You can't build a ramp that way," he said. "It'll never work." And with that, he took Evan to Home Depot, got a bunch of wood and the two of them, along with Anna, built a ramp for racing toy cars. Peter used it as an opportunity to teach them about the Pythagorean theorem, which I knew had something to do with right angles. It took most of the day. I brought a tray of sandwiches and lemonade out to the three of them at lunchtime, but stayed back, watching them laugh and chat around the picnic table. I took photos so they would remember this special day with their dad. A day he didn't work, didn't even try. And after the ramp was built I painted it, each lane a different color, and in black along its side the words *Built By The World's Greatest Dad*. Good god, I think, we can't split up. I can't bear the thought of it, can't even begin to face all the attendant fear and guilt. I'm already thinking about how it will kill me for this woman he's seeing to be my kids' stepmother. I'm a thousand steps ahead of what's actually occurring at this moment.

"Can you tell me, at least, who it is?" I ask Peter. He pauses and says, "You don't know her. It's someone I went to law school with."

I wasn't expecting that. I was expecting a paralegal or a secretary or an associate. Or a client. Or a client's wife. But not a law school classmate. "What?" I say, dumbfounded.

Law school feels like it happened a lifetime ago, but in reality, it's been twelve years since Peter graduated. I remember it vaguely, a three-year blur of cold New Hampshire winters, a small apartment a few blocks from Franklin Pierce Law Center and its intellectual property law program. I had a four-hour-a-day round-trip commute to my job at Harvard Business School, where I was the secretary for three professors (we were given the generous title of "faculty assistant") until being promoted to research assistant. Peter's commute was a mere four blocks to school, but he was never home between classes. Instead he was studying, or working at the law review office, or at his various part-time jobs. He was an on-campus LexisNexis representative, a clerk for a while at the office of a divorce attorney, and a barista several mornings a week at a local coffee shop.

On weekends, while he continued his fifteen-to-eighteen-hour days of studying, attending classes, and working, I was alone. My friends were a five-hour drive away, in New York and New Jersey, and all my new friends were really Peter's—other law students and their spouses. So I went hiking, visited cider mills, pumpkin fields, bookstores, antiques shops, and small towns in New Hampshire and Vermont. I learned how Shaker furniture was made, peered at hand-blown glass pitchers through the window of the Simon Pearce glass factory, and taught myself to bake all kinds of bread, kneading it by hand. I tried to write, but I was too lonely and depressed to do more than vent in my journal.

Peter's life was different. He had a purpose—he was here to attend law school. And he had a social life. He was back in graduate school again and, even at the ripe age of thirty, easily slipped back into that world: the intense studying and obsessing over exams and grades but also parties and booze and weed to combat the stress. He went to parties I didn't attend because I didn't feel welcome (and didn't want to spend the night listening to them complain about professors and classes and applying for summer jobs). Peter put together a cover band, Blackacre (which is, actually, a legal term), composed of students—with him on bass—that performed at house parties and a local bar. Remembering that now suddenly brings me back to the night we told his law school friends that I was pregnant. It was between sets at a bar where Blackacre was playing. Peter and I sat in a booth with a group of his classmates, everyone drinking beer but me; I was nursing a ginger ale. After Peter said we were having a baby, our little crowd cheered and whooped and toasted us. And I remember Peter's broad smile, his arm around my shoulders giving me a proud squeeze. I felt lucky and loved and happy.

And at that memory my mind goes back to another night, one a few months earlier. It was Valentine's Day, the best one I ever had or will ever have, I imagine. That morning—with my period nine days late—I decided to do a pregnancy test. I had miscarried a few months earlier and I wanted this test to be positive, wanted it so badly that my legs were shaking. I had to leave the bathroom while the little test strip did its work. When I walked back in and saw the result was positive, I started jumping up and down, silently, so I wouldn't wake Peter. It was only five-thirty A.M. and I had a long commute into Boston ahead of me. But later in the evening, when he finally got home from school and slid into bed next to me, I rolled to face him. "Guess what," I said, without waiting for a reply. "I'm pregnant! Happy Valentine's Day!"

Peter smiled, slowly, and at that moment, I believed I could read his mind, feel his pleasure at seeing our intention take shape. It worked—sex really worked!—we were pregnant. "Wow, really?" he asked. "You did a test?"

"Yep," I said. "Can you believe it?" I was so happy I couldn't lie still, couldn't contain my excitement. Peter hugged me from behind, scooping me up inside his solid frame and laughing at me as I wriggled around, squealing with joy. "I love you," he said, and kissed my head. "I love you too," I'd answered. And I meant it. Our daughter was born the following autumn.

We left New Hampshire within days of his May 1997 graduation—Peter was number one in his law school class, editor of the intellectual property law review and he gave an excellent valedictory speech at the ceremony—and that was the end of law school. We moved to San Diego with our baby girl. I hardly thought about law school again.

"Is it Melissa? Todd's wife?" I ask, still not looking at him but wanting to know the name of my nemesis. She had her second child a few weeks before I had Anna, although she was ten years my junior.

No, Peter says, it's not Melissa. "What made you think of her?"

"I don't know. You used to say she was cute. And she and Todd split up after law school, don't you remember?"

"Oh yeah," Peter says. "But no, it's not someone you know."

"What's her name?" I ask.

Peter is pained. "Eilene, it doesn't matter. You don't know her. I don't want to tell you her name." But I need her name to make her real.

"She's out here then? In San Diego or L.A.?" I've been a reporter for twenty-some-odd years, I'm going to keep pushing until I get some information.

"No. She's in New York City," Peter says.

Oh, the beauty of business trips, I think. You can have a girlfriend on the East Coast and a wife on the west one. Now I'm crying in addition to shaking.

"Eilene," Peter says, "I thought you hated being married to me. You hate living with me. You're miserable. I thought you wanted a way out."

The fact is, he's right. I do hate being married to him. I do want a way out. I just wanted the way out to be through a door we opened together, not this. We have two wonderful children and I believe they deserve to have their parents together while they are growing up. Sure, divorce is common, but that doesn't mean many divorced parents don't feel guilty about changing the game for their kids. And then there is the economics of a divorce and how the disparity in our respective incomes—I'm not even sure at this point exactly how much Peter earns each month—will play out.

These days I work about twenty-five to thirty hours a week. Last year my income was about one-tenth what Peter says he earned. My best year as a writer I earned $60,000. It was during the dot-com boom, when business magazines were three hundred pages thick and webzines that would last six months were paying two dollars a word. I wrote constantly, every second my kids were either in preschool or asleep. I wound up in physical therapy to treat carpal tunnel and a frozen shoulder. That's what a financially great year looks like for me.

Still, Peter expects me to earn my keep and pay a certain portion of the household bills, which I do. At the same time, he reminds me regularly how hard he works and how many of the bills *he* pays. On weekends, Peter doesn't participate much in family life, whether that's making a meal or handling a playdate. He usually just holes up in his garage office—a converted laundry room—where he is ostensibly working, but in reality, he's more apt to be listening to music, shopping for tech stuff, or watching porn. Last year Anna walked into his office on a Sunday morning without knocking and caught her first glimpse of a blow job, happening in living color on her father's computer screen. He later told me he was getting rid of junk mail while doing other work, and he likes to make sure it's junk before he deletes it. (My hunch is the subject line probably made clear what it was.) He'll walk in from the garage when we're having lunch and if I ask him, "Can you spend some time with the kids?" he'll say, "I'm working. Someone's got to pay the mortgage."

Our mutual resentment (I call it our "suffering contest") has been snowballing for the past five or six years, each of us now living largely separate lives, sharing less. We can be in the same room and not speak or look at each other, and it isn't the kind of comfortable silence that comes from years of mutual love and friendship. It is a brooding silence, wrought of anger and hurt and exhaustion. Our marriage has become a business partnership—we are raising our kids and managing a household, but we don't love each other anymore.

This year on Peter's forty-sixth birthday I took him out to dinner at George's, a restaurant in La Jolla with spectacular views of the coast. He was tired so I kept making conversation, talking about Anna and Evan, other people we knew, an article I'd just read in the *New Yorker*. Finally, I said, "Why don't you say something? I am doing all the talking." I hadn't yet learned to be okay with silence, so I always filled in the spaces. Peter said he preferred when I did the talking. "All I'm going to do is complain about work," he said. He seemed sad. I didn't know it then, but he had just begun his affair.

It's nearly six A.M. and the morning light is starting to seep in through the blinds; the kids are stirring in their rooms. Peter gets up and throws on a T-shirt and some sweats. He almost never gets up with our children, even on the weekends, so we decide to tell them I was up all night with a stomach bug, and I'm resting before we go to the beach, which was my plan for the day. I hadn't known if Peter would join us or not.

He stands at the edge of the bed, his hands on the wooden footboard as if it's a ship's railing, leaning over slightly to look at the ocean—rather than the rug beneath our bed—before he sails away.

I'm still curled into a ball, wanting to sleep and pretend this isn't happening. "Why didn't you go in-house? Why wouldn't you try to work for a company instead of a firm? If you'd worked less, maybe we would have stood a chance," I say. Peter leans forward, still holding on to the footboard.

"That's one thing that's true," he says. "You did ask me to go in-house, I know, but I didn't want to be an in-house counsel. I wanted to be a partner, a partner in a law firm." He pauses. "I'm more ambitious than I thought I was."

I can hear our son moving around his room. "Why did you start sleeping with someone else? Why didn't you tell me? We could go to counseling, we could at least try again," I say.

Peter takes a breath and purses his lips in the way he always does when he is thinking about what to say next. "Because we were stuck and we were miserable and I couldn't see any way to change things. I didn't know how we were going to get out of it. So I pulled the trigger," he says.

Starting a relationship with someone else while still coming home to your wife, your dinner waiting for you, your kids bathed and in their pajamas, ready for you to lie down next to them and smell their shampooed hair and tuck them in, that's called "pulling a trigger"? It's not called lying anymore? When did the names of things become so easy to change? I'm so angry and yet so brokenhearted that I will spend the next two months in bed, crying.

"I knew if I pulled it," Peter says, "we couldn't go back."

THREE

October 2011

I'M DRIVING TO PICK up Anna and Evan from Peter's new house, which I haven't seen yet, in Del Mar, a posh beach town off U.S. Highway 101. It's a twenty-five-minute drive from my neighborhood, Del Cerro, where Peter and I lived together before our divorce. We separated in 2009 and officially divorced five months ago, in May. I stayed married so I could remain on Peter's health insurance but also because he didn't want us to rush into divorce. Who knew how we might feel after a year of separation? he said many times. In the end, though, I decided I didn't want to be married any longer, found health insurance I could afford, and filed the papers. By that time Peter was house shopping, and this was the one he wanted. He knew it the second he set eyes on it, in June. Two million dollars' worth of wood, glass, concrete, and steel overlooking the state beach and a pristine lagoon down the hill. Peter negotiated for a while with the owners, who were asking more than he could afford. I'm not sure he could afford what he wound up paying, which I only know because my kids have told me, and why they know, I'm not sure.

In fact, somehow they know how much everything in Peter's new house costs, from the dining room table fashioned out of a single piece of wood ($7,000), to the direct-from-Italy espresso maker ($900). Peter waited out the owners of the house, anxious about losing it but willing to gamble, and in the end, he won, borrowing money from his retirement savings to make the down payment.

The sale closed in late September, and for the last six weeks, Anna and Evan have been staying there on the nights they spend with Peter. Tonight, Anna asked me to pick her and Evan up so I could come inside, see their bedrooms, and get a grand tour.

I've got the car windows open to the early October air and I'm thinking about birthdays. Soon Evan and Anna will turn fourteen and sixteen—their birthdays are two days apart. It's hard to believe Peter and I, who've known each other since we were twenty-three, are now forty-eight and forty-nine years old. The night before each child's birthday I usually decorate the dining room in some theme: fairies, Harry Potter, race cars, sports. I hang streamers, make a big Happy Birthday sign and attach cutouts to fishing wire hung from the ceiling, so that the football players or fairies seem to be floating in the air. I love to watch my kids' faces when they come into the dining room before school. Then I let them have a slice of cake with breakfast.

As I drive, I'm figuring out whether or not Anna and Evan will be at my house the day before their birthdays, and I realize Anna won't be and my heart sinks. I don't want to miss that morning with her, when she wakes up as a sixteen-year-old. I can't think of how to be there if she's at Peter's, but I push it out of my mind and focus on the road, turning to parallel the ocean and the setting sun.

The house where I live became mine as part of our divorce settlement. One Saturday morning about a year ago, though, Peter came by to drop off something one of our kids left at his place. At that point he was living in a rented two-bedroom condo in Solana Beach, another town a few miles north of where he is now. He arrived aggravated and angry about having to spend an hour driving back and forth when he had other things to do. I walked him to his car as he was leaving so we could talk out of earshot of the kids and he stopped by the side gate to light a cigarette. He wanted to calm down and needed the forced deep breaths that smoking necessitated to do that. It didn't seem to be working.

He was furious that I had insisted he knock on the front door and allow us to let him in, rather than using his "emergency" key. "You want me to knock on my own fucking door?" he said. "You've got to be kidding." He took another drag. "You know how much equity I put into that house for you?" he asked, pointing the hand with the cigarette toward the front door.

Over time he got used to knocking and now has a house again, his dream house, the one that has just come into view. It is imposing, made of squares and rectangles, a gray, speckled cinderblock wall hiding the big yard from view, except for a very small, cinderblock-size window. The way to the front door is through a locked gate.

Fortunately I have rehearsed these first moments in my mind. I will be impressed, for the sake of my kids (and also genuinely, in all likelihood). I have a cup of jasmine green tea in my travel mug to give me something to sip if I feel like crying (or screaming). I remind myself why I'm doing this tour—my kids live here some of the time and they are proud of it, and they want me to be part of that.

I can already hear Anna and Evan yelling at me from above, so

I get out of the car, close the door, and look up. They are on the roof with Peter; they're waving and yelling to me. "Mom! Mommy! We'll be right down! We'll let you in!" I know the gate code, but I wait for them to open it from the other side.

There is a click as they unlock it, and then my kids are in front of me, jumping around with excitement. "Hi, Mom!" Evan says and gives me a clinging hug, and I want to just bury my face in his hair and keep him with me, not have him be in this house that feels too fancy and rich for any of us, including Peter. *Especially* Peter, who grew up in a house owned by the church for which his father worked, around the corner from public housing projects. Peter, who went to a pricey private school in the suburbs on a full-ride, low-income scholarship. Peter, who started working when he was still in grammar school, delivering newspapers in the freezing cold, who spent his free time in high school stocking shelves and cleaning floors at Tops supermarket. Peter, who worked his way through college and graduate school making and delivering pizza in Ithaca, New York.

Now, walking on the concrete path embedded in the wide green lawn, past the large fountain in the center where water gently rolls down wavy white columns and the smell of salt water infuses the air, I can see how hard he is working to create a life that is a million miles from the one he left in upstate New York.

He is waving to me from the roof, pulling the bill of his New York Knicks hat up so he can see me bearing witness to this new, more sophisticated life, the trimmings of which I'm about to see: heavy modern furniture from stores I didn't even know existed; cupboards packed full of Whole Foods groceries, bottles of expensive wines, top-shelf vodka and tequila and special glasses from which to drink them; art purchased not just because it's pretty but because it's also an investment; silverware from a special silver maker in Santa Fe, New Mexico; pots and pans so heavy and serious-looking, you feel you're a better cook just by holding them.

I wave back, taking in the surroundings. The house sits on a hill, and from the amount of construction going on, it seems like the neighbors are trying to one-up each other with glass-fronted additions that reach higher and higher into the sky, angling for as much of the ocean view as space will allow.

I walk through the front door and see the room to my right. It has a concrete floor with an area rug over it. It's not furnished yet, but there are the full-length glass window-doors I've heard so much about, the ones that slide noiselessly open to the backyard.

"Mom!" Anna yells. "Look at this. . . ." and she rolls the glass doors open. "Isn't this so cool?" Yes, I'm thinking, it is so cool. Evan's band could practice here, instead of in my hot, stuffy garage with the door closed so the neighbors don't complain.

"Yeah, that's incredible!" I say, thinking if they gave Academy Awards for best actress-in-a-divorce, I would win, no contest. That's how genuine I think I'm being. That's how excited I am pretending to be. It's hard for me to focus, however, because my mind is a million steps ahead of me, thinking about how my kids will never again have a sleepover or party or band practice at my house. That soon they will be spending more and more time at Dad's, opting for the half-mile walk to boogie board at Torrey Pines State Beach rather than the quarter-mile walk up to the strip mall in our neighborhood for groceries at Windmill Farms and tacos at Guadalupe's.

"Careful, Anna, roll it back slowly," Peter cautions, as the window-doors are closed and we head upstairs for the rest of the tour. "Careful on the stairs," Peter says quietly to me. "Bamboo is kind of slippery." Being considerate of the unblemished floors, I have taken off my shoes and am padding around in socks. But Peter is right, the wood is completely smooth even though I can see the narrow, individual planks. In the waning sunlight, it is the color of pale honey. I look out over the living area, one big room essentially, that contains the kitchen, the dining area, and the living room. Peter takes me through the kitchen, pointing out all the unusual flourishes, like a spice drawer with wooden cutouts for each bottle, and the recessed warming drawer, a metal compartment next to the oven that exists solely to keep food warm.

Peter tells me most of the furniture is from one store. "I don't have time to be constantly shopping around, it's too much. I liked all the furniture at this one place, so I worked with a decorator there," he says.

The furniture, although new, looks oddly familiar. After we leave the living room and head down the hall, I figure out why. It looks like a high-priced law firm waiting area. Everything in muted blues, grays, and browns, the leather furniture heavy and solid and serious.

The kids run ahead, down the hall to Anna's room. One of its walls is painted a deep, vivid pink. The queen-size bed frame, Anna tells me, is made from the wood of recycled train tracks. From India. I wonder if the fuel required to import them from India cancels out any environmental gain from recycling the wood, but don't say it. Peter is standing beyond the door's threshold, smiling at Anna, then looking at me. She lies languidly on her bed, illustrating the different ways its size—unlike her twin bed at my house—allows her to stretch out. "You can jump on it too," she says.

"No, you can't," says Peter, and I laugh.

Now we're in the hall bathroom, and I'm getting a demonstration of the gravity-defying sink. The water stays within the confines of the sink's implausibly shallow basin, although it appears it will spill over any second. "Look, Mom, look at this. Look how cool this is," Anna says.

"Wow, that is amazing!" I say, sounding like a kindergarten teacher. Evan shows me again. "But look here, Mom, look under here," he says. "It's leaking." And sure enough, water is slowly dripping from a tiny space where the pipes join into a plastic cup beneath the sink. Evan is always on the lookout for potential disasters.

"I've got to get that fixed," Peter adds.

We move to the last room in the hallway, the master bedroom. There's Peter's bed, a California king, simple and elegant, with matching side tables, matching side lamps, and a fantastic mid-century modern dresser he bought from the previous owners. It's hard to look at the bed, knowing he is having sex in it. Probably a lot of sex. Peter is cycling through various girlfriends, all younger than he is, whom he meets on Match.com.

"Mom, look how big this closet is!" Anna pulls me toward the walk-in closet, with shelves so high, even six-foot-tall Peter has to stand on a step stool to reach the one at the very top. And then we turn around to face the bathroom, the *pièce de résistance,* with its magnificent centerpiece: a sleek modern version of a claw-footed tub, only without the claw feet. It's so smooth and white it could be made of alabaster, carved by some Italian artist. There's the same crazy-shaped sink as the one in the hall bathroom, only twice as wide. The shower looks the same too, only bigger and with a high-tech showerhead. Peter sees me peering at it. "I wanted a really strong stream, you know, because my back always hurts." I nod. "Of course," I say. In a corner of the shower I can see a bottle of women's shampoo and what looks like a bar of fancy soap, the kind that has pieces of oatmeal or flecks of lavender in it.

Finally, the kids have had enough. My tea is lukewarm, the sun has set, it's time to go. We all walk back down the hallway into the kitchen. "Mom, you didn't see the roof!" Anna says. "Next time," I say.

"Can we go up there now, Daddy? Can we show Mommy the roof?" I look at Peter, hoping he can see how tired I feel. He does. "Let's wait until it's daytime and Mommy can get the full view, okay?" Anna sighs. "Whatever," she says.

The kids run down to their rooms to grab their backpacks and everything else they've brought with them for the weekend. Peter is standing behind the large center island, fiddling with a knob on the stove top. "So what do you think?" he asks, looking up at me. "Really, isn't it so me? It's like the perfect house for me, isn't it?" He is looking at me so clear-eyed, so earnestly. I can feel the anxiety and envy and fear in my chest relax a little, at least temporarily. Why Peter wants my approval I'll never know, but he does, and so I give it. He is always so sure of himself, of his decisions, always the smartest guy in the room. Should he go to law school? Yes. Should we buy a house? Yes. Send the kids to private school? Absolutely. Roth IRA or iBonds? IBonds. When my editor at *The New York Times* offered me the chance to do a monthly column, it was Peter who convinced me to take it. "What if I don't have enough time for it each month, because of the kids or other work? I'm not sure I can handle it," I had said. Peter didn't hesitate. "You should definitely do it. It'll be important for your career, and you can do it. You never miss deadlines, and you won't now." He sounded so confident in my abilities that I took it on. And he was right, it opened up other opportunities for me.

Which means that even though I loathe his arrogance, I also count on it. I count on Peter to know the answers. Lots of people count on him for that; it's what lawyers and scientists and scientists-turned-lawyers do—they give us the answers.

"It is, Peter, it really is," I say. And I mean it. This house is totally his taste, sleek and modern and spare and cold. And expensive.

"You would have liked this, wouldn't you? If we were still together?" he asks.

It's a statement that's simultaneously heartbreaking and nasty, him needing me to tell him this was the right thing to do while letting me know that if I'd just been a better wife, all this could have been mine too. Was it the right thing to do? To buy a house he couldn't afford, that will just tie him more tightly to a job he hates? I feel exhausted. "I don't know," I say, being vague. "It's beautiful, of course, but I like places that are a little cozier. It definitely fits you though. I can really see you here."

I start heading down the stairs and call for the kids. "Okay, okay!" they scream, running to the front door. I pack their stuff into my Prius, and they spend a few minutes hugging Peter and saying goodbye and telling him what a great weekend they had. My window is rolled down and Peter leans into it. "Thanks for coming up to get them and see the house," he says. We are being uncharacteristically kind to each other tonight. "I wanted to," I say. "I'm really glad I got to see it. It's beautiful. And the kids love it." He raps on the windows in the back as a goodbye to all of us.

It's dark as I back out of the driveway and the house's outdoor lights come on, illuminating the tufted seagrass out front, the small palm trees, the enormous garage door, the gray cinderblock wall. Peter is in the kitchen, and from the outside it is a sweet scene of domesticity—the couch, the silver lamp that curves over it, the dining table beyond, Peter opening cabinets to rustle up some dinner for himself—all of it silhouetted against a muted yellow light. Unlike the past two years, when Peter rented small apartments and condos that came furnished, he owns this house, one he believes reflects who he is or, perhaps, who he aspires to be.

Regardless, he won't be moving year to year anymore, and that means Anna and Evan won't have to continually readjust. Now the three of them have a home; they have stability. It feels like a new beginning, for him and for all of us.

■ FOUR

Labor Day Weekend 2014

THREE YEARS LATER ANNA is starting college and we are headed, as a family, to move-in weekend at the University of Michigan. Anna, Evan, and I are on the sidewalk in front of my house, ten bags of luggage—eight of them Anna's—lined up neatly on the driveway. I imagine we look like a vacationing family that's been abandoned in the middle of suburbia. We are waiting for Peter to pick us up and take all of us to the airport, where we will board a plane bound for Ann Arbor.

It's the edge of a holiday weekend—the Wednesday before Labor Day—and the airport will likely be a zoo. Peter is already half an hour late. "We're going to miss the plane!" Anna shouts at no one, furious and teary-eyed. We crane our collective necks to the right, aiming to see around the corner and spot Peter's black Tiguan. Finally, there is the unmistakable sound of tires skidding on gravel to announce his arrival, and then the car is racing up the driveway, nearly hitting the luggage before Peter brakes.

"You were supposed to be here thirty minutes ago. What the hell?" I say, flinging bags into the back of the car. "Dad, we're going to miss our flight!" Anna shouts.

"We're fine," Peter says, oddly upbeat even though it's barely seven A.M. and he is not a morning person. He and Evan are taking out the bags I've thrown in and reorganizing them so they fit. Anna is brooding and anxious and excited all at the same time. "Let's go, let's go!" she says.

The car is so crammed full of luggage that my son is sitting in the trunk area, wedged between a gigantic blue duffel bag and a red suitcase. I can't even see Anna across the backseat, buried as we are beneath bags of clothes, toiletries, and all the other stuff she is taking with her. Peter offered to drive—and he has the biggest car so it made sense—but with all the luggage that needs to be checked, I am worried we really may miss the flight. I can't find the seat belt so I am hanging on to a suitcase during what is becoming one of the wildest rides of my life. Peter is driving 85 MPH on side streets. Then he's on the freeway, cutting everyone off and weaving in and out of lanes as he flies toward the airport. I have never seen him drive like this, but I haven't driven with him in about a year. Anna and I get motion sick easily, but he's taking no prisoners this morning. In the last year or so he's become increasingly short-tempered, and I am afraid to say anything that might set him off, so I just hold on.

He is about to make a left turn onto the Pacific Coast Highway, which parallels the airport, only he's in the rightmost lane of three, a lane that has a right arrow painted down its center to make it clear to drivers there is only one option. It feels like a kind of fever dream as I watch Peter cut across two lanes of traffic to make the left, while everyone around us is leaning on their horns and giving him the finger. He just keeps going, eyes straight ahead. I look at Evan, but he's got his eyes closed. Peter screeches up to the airport's valet parking—three times what it would cost to park in the regular lot—gets out of the car, and lights a cigarette. I peel myself out of the backseat and walk over to the luggage carts.

"I'm never driving with you again, ever," I say, realizing at the same time I will have to drive with him for the next four days. "What?" Peter says, taking a deep drag of his just-lit cigarette and shrugging. "We made it, right? And in plenty of time."

He stands there looking past me, in his leather jacket and T-shirt and his tan Lululemon lounge pants, sucking hard on the cigarette before tossing it to the ground and crushing it. "Are you out of your mind?" I ask, as Anna and Evan load up the luggage carts. "You almost killed us." Peter laughs at me, at crazy, overly cautious Eilene. This is why I left you, he seems to be saying. Always making something out of nothing. So rigid. So afraid.

Somehow things work out. We get all ten pieces of luggage checked, make the plane, and later that night are in Detroit, waiting on a long line to rent an SUV before finally settling into our rooms at America's Best Value Inn—the cheapest hotel Peter could find, at $65 a night. It is not such a great value, however, with its tiny rooms and stained, cardboard-thick walls. This first night Peter is sharing a room with Evan; I am sharing this one with Anna. Tomorrow, when we get to Ann Arbor, Evan will stay with me, and Peter will have his own room, in case he needs to work. Anna won't need to share a room with any of us, as she will be spending her first night in a college dormitory.

"This is kind of gross," Anna says, poking her head into the closet-size bathroom.

"It's one night," Peter says. "You'll survive."

The next morning, we head to the Ann Arbor Target, along with ten million other out-of-town parents, to buy the things our budding undergrad will need to survive dorm life. We start wheeling our cart up and down aisles, grabbing plastic storage bins, school supplies, extra-long dorm-bed-size sheets, putting them in the cart until it's clear we'll need another cart. Evan has left and headed to the electronics department and Peter has abandoned us briefly to get a gigantic diet soda. He finds us putting a collapsible clothes hamper in the cart. "I can't shop anymore," he says. "I'm tired."

"I know, but we're getting there," I say.

"Daddy, come on, it's not taking that long," Anna says.

But Peter has had it and sits down on a big blue bean bag chair in the college furniture section, leans his head back, and closes his eyes. "I'm just going to sit here. Get me when you have what you need." There is a part of me that feels as I did in marriage, that I should let him sleep because he's paying for all of this, and he's clearly dead tired from working so much. And there is a part of me that thinks: If I have to do this, he does too. But Anna looks almost relieved that he's going to sit out the shopping frenzy. Now she can take her time without worrying that Peter is bored or itching to get back to the hotel for a nap. He can just nap right here, in the middle of Target.

"Okay," I say. "We'll be back in twenty minutes." I see Evan walking toward us. He sees his father trying to nap in the bean bag chair, so he flops down on one nearby and puts on headphones. Half an hour later, with two full carts, we are back in the furniture area. Evan unplugs his headphones. "Is Daddy asleep?" I ask, looking at Peter. I can't tell if he's just resting his eyes or if he's really out.

"Yeah, I think so," Evan says. "He hasn't been up since you left." I shake Peter's arm gently and call his name. Then a little harder. He opens his eyes slowly, so deep in sleep I can see he's struggling to surface; he keeps getting pulled back under. "Peter?" I say, more loudly. "Peter, we're done. We're ready to check out. You okay?"

He nods yes, then shakes his head a little to snap out of the fog and runs a hand up and down his face. "Okay, okay, I'm up," he says, rising with difficulty from the low-slung chair and reaching down to grab his watery soda. After cashing out, we head to the Ann Arbor Regent Hotel. At two P.M., Anna's designated "move-in" time, the four of us drive to the brick buildings known as East Quad to unload our daughter and all her belongings. Peter and Evan make trips up and down stairs with the contents of the car while I help Anna unpack her clothes and make up her bed, which is lofted above her desk. She is rushing me along, telling me she'll finish up, it's fine, it's fine. She's desperate for us to leave so she can get ready to go out and begin her college life in earnest. There are some girls she's met waiting in the hallway to hang out with her, and their parents have already left. So Evan, Peter, and I say our goodbyes on the dorm steps and head to town for dinner. Our plan for this weekend is to get to know Ann Arbor tomorrow, maybe try and get Anna to have one more meal with us, and then on Saturday we will attend the university's first football game of the season (without Anna, who will be sitting in the student section). The game was actually Peter's idea.

We walk around Main Street, Liberty Street, and Washtenaw Avenue looking for a place to eat. Evan suggests Five Guys Burgers, so that's where we land. Since finishing up at the dorm, Peter has been listless and pale. I think that maybe he just needs some red meat, or anything that's full of iron and fat. He's thin and shaky and completely exhausted. It's not even a particularly cool night, but he's got his leather jacket zipped up. "Are you okay?" I ask him. "Are you feeling sick?" He looks like he might have a fever or the chills.

"No, I'm fine," he says. "Just wiped out from moving Anna in."

I order Evan and Peter burgers and fries and get a veggie burger for myself. We eat silently. It seems it's taking all of Peter's energy and focus just to chew and swallow. "Do you want another? Either of you?" I ask, looking from one to the other. Evan says yes, so Peter says he'll have one, too, and I go to the counter and order each of them another cheeseburger. I would order Peter three if he would eat them. I look back at the two of them in the booth, introverted in similar ways, starting to chat a little as I wait for my turn at the counter. Beneath the table I can see Peter's bony white ankles peeking out from beneath his pant legs, unexpectedly fragile.

The next morning my phone starts buzzing at six A.M. It's a text from Peter. Evan is asleep in the other bed.

"You up?" his message says.

"Yes, are you working?" I can't imagine any other reason he would be up this early. Peter is the type of person that has to set two or three alarms to go off at five-minute intervals to compensate for how often he hits the snooze button. But for work, he'll get up. The guy rarely took a night feeding when our kids were babies, but if there was a two A.M. conference call, he was on it.

"Actually, I'm in a cab on the way to the airport. Something is blowing up at work."

I reread it several times.

"Are you kidding?" I text back. "You are taking a flight back to San Diego right now?"

"Yes, I have to. It's work. I'm sorry."

I look over at Evan, sleeping. I'm not even angry, I'm confused. I don't understand what is happening. Peter is not down the hall; he is on his way to the airport? I pull back the covers as quietly as I can, tiptoe out into the bathroom, close the door, and call him.

"Hey," he answers.

"Peter, what about the game tomorrow? What about Evan? You were supposed to do this with us. You were the one who suggested it. You bought the tickets! And what about the car? It's rented in your name. And I can't afford to pay for it. What is going on? You are leaving?"

I am bone-tired already and the day hasn't even begun. Why is there always a work crisis?

"Eilene," Peter says, calmly. "Do you think I *want* to leave? I *have* to. It's *my* client. I'm the partner that's responsible for what happens and there's a problem and so I'm going back now. I'll get it taken care of, and I'll be on a red-eye back to Detroit tonight."

"This is insane," I say. "It's the Friday of Labor Day weekend and you're telling me that there's a problem with one of your clients and there is no one else, not one single attorney in the entire San Diego office, that can handle it for you? Do they know you are taking your daughter to college for the first time? Did you tell them that?"

Peter blows air loudly out of his mouth, an angry sigh. I know he is rolling his eyes.

"Eilene, there's nothing I can do, I'm sorry. I feel really bad. But I have to handle this."

"Okay," I say. "But you can't miss the game, Peter, I'm serious. You can't disappoint Evan. He's looking forward to it and you guys don't do many things together."

Peter assures me he, too, is looking forward to it. That he really wants to go. It'll be fun, he says. "I promise, I will be on a plane to Michigan tonight. I'll get back at six A.M., I'll sleep for a few hours, and then we'll go to the game together. I didn't even check out because I'm coming back."

He always finds some way to avoid being a parent, I think. The three of us were supposed to explore Ann Arbor today. My son doesn't want to hang out with me all day, he was looking forward to time with his father, to Peter actually being here and doing things with him. I was hoping I might get some of my freelance assignments done while the two of them spent time together meandering around, chatting, shopping at the M Den. I have a bunch of looming deadlines. But Peter has to work and his work has always—and will always—be more important than mine. He reminds me regularly that I need his financial support to live in San Diego. The recurring message is clear: *We may not be married anymore, but you still need me.* I'm already so sick of this trip and of move-in weekend and of my daughter's embarrassment at having parents. I want to go home too.

"If you miss the game, Peter . . ." I say, trailing off.

"I will be there," he insists. "I promise."

When Evan wakes up, I break the news to him that Peter had to go back to San Diego, but just for the day, and that he'll be on his way back to Ann Arbor tonight.

"He's not coming back," Evan says flatly. He isn't even looking at me. He's just sitting up against the headboard, staring at some spot above the television mounted on the wall across from him. Peter doesn't do so many of the things he says he wants to do with Evan—like watching his band perform, going for a bike ride or a run on the weekend, watching a ball game—that Evan has stopped counting on his father to actually do anything he says he'll do. There is always an excuse, Evan has told me. And it's almost always work.

"Look at me," I say. "He *wants* to go to the game; he's very upset he has to leave today. He will be here tomorrow morning. He promised. He's taking a red-eye tonight."

"Mom," Evan says, turning his eyes to mine. "He's not coming back."

At 10:45 that night, my phone rings with a call from Peter. His flight was supposed to have left fifteen minutes ago. I pick up. "I missed the flight," he says. Evan is in the bed next to me, reading ESPN on his laptop. I glance at him but he refuses to look up.

"Peter," I say into my phone. "You promised."

"Would you listen to me? I'm *at the airport*. They wouldn't *let me on the plane*. They have some rule now that they close the doors twenty minutes before takeoff, and if you're not at the gate you can't get on the plane. It's fucking bullshit."

I can't believe this. I can't believe Evan was right.

"How late were you getting to the gate?" I ask, trying to find a way to excuse this, some way to explain this to Evan.

"I got here just as they closed the cabin doors. I always used to be able to get here fifteen minutes before takeoff, and it was no problem getting on the plane."

I can't remember a time when you could get to an airport gate just fifteen minutes before the plane is set to depart and expect to be allowed on, at least not in the post-9/11 world. Months from now, Peter will tell me a story about a business trip to Pittsburgh he had recently taken. On the way back to San Diego, he and a colleague were running late and when Peter reached the gate, he demanded the agents hold the plane because his colleague was, at that very moment, racing through the airport to meet him and make this flight. When the agents refused, he became indignant.

"They couldn't hold the plane for two minutes?" he will ask me, although I won't be expected to answer. "Come on, *two fucking minutes*? She was right behind me."

In what world is it reasonable to ask a pilot to reopen doors that have already been locked and secured? To interrupt flight attendants getting the cabin ready for takeoff? I will tell you in what world—the world of an addict, where the absurd seems reasonable and can even be convincingly rationalized, not just to themselves but to those around them.

With addiction, the value of drugs becomes overblown at the expense of other things that really are important, says Rita Goldstein, a professor of psychiatry at the Icahn School of Medicine in New York City, well known for her studies of cocaine addiction. "An addict will tell you they love their children, their spouse, their work, but that these can wait. The need to consume drugs cannot wait," she says. "There is a change in how things are valued, with the brain needing the drug more than anything else." For someone with a cocaine addiction—which I will learn is one of the drugs Peter is using regularly—the part of the brain that monitors errors becomes smaller and doesn't function well, says Goldstein. That might have been why Peter didn't think it was a mistake to leave his family to feed his drug habit. He didn't realize he was doing anything wrong.

But I didn't know that then, in Ann Arbor, when I was angry at Peter's colleagues for insisting he fly back right away and handle whatever issue had arisen. I didn't have the slightest understanding of any of this that weekend in 2014. I thought Peter was telling the truth. I couldn't see any reason why he wouldn't have wanted to be at that football game with us. The morning after Peter misses his flight, Evan and I, along with a whole bunch of families staying in the hotel, hop on the shuttle bus to the Big House—the name of Michigan's massive stadium—where we will watch the university's football team crush Appalachian State.

Evan and I sit steaming in the ninety-degree heat and humidity with 110,000 drunk, rabid Michigan fans screaming "Go Blue!" at the top of their lungs. It becomes a thunderous background noise to everything else happening around us—the colorful inflated beach balls making their way around the stadium, spontaneous eruptions of "the wave," announcers emphatically calling plays, the smell of hot dogs and nachos, popcorn and spilled beer. I send Peter some photos of the field, an ocean of blue and yellow clothing, pom-poms, hats, face paint, hair—you name it, it is blue and yellow. I send him photos of Evan and me there, without him. That is the essential message of my texts: *You are not here. And you promised to be.*

That night, after we've packed up, we head down the hall to Peter's room (he left a card key for me at the desk, just in case) to pack up his things, strewn about as he rushed out the door and into the waiting cab. I feel like I'm doing something I shouldn't be, violating Peter's privacy, but I remind myself he asked me to get his things. He brought only a few pieces of clothing with him and those are still in his bag. Otherwise it's a bunch of uneaten protein bars and candy lying on the bureau; in the bathroom, a razor, some pricey shave gel from Kiehl's, a bottle of Advil, and a small container of Tums tablets. We throw them into his blue duffel bag, which will go with us to the airport.

It's a warm, breezy night in San Diego when we land. Peter picks us up, running late, as usual. I notice again that he is wearing the heavy leather jacket and jeans; Evan and I are in shorts and T-shirts. I climb into the front seat of the Tiguan, spacious again without all of Anna's luggage. Evan isn't in the car yet; he's putting our bags into the trunk.

"I can't believe you didn't come back," I say quietly to Peter. I notice a half-full pack of cigarettes lying inside a compartment in the center console and a large sweaty soda in the cup holder. "Evan said you wouldn't come back, but like an idiot, I believed you."

Peter rolls his eyes. "You don't know how bad I felt about missing the flight. I felt terrible." I want to snap back that I don't care how bad *he* felt, I care how bad our son felt, but at that moment Evan enters the backseat and straps himself in. Peter glances in the rearview mirror, then turns in his seat to face his son. "I'm really sorry, buddy," he says. "I really wanted to be there." His tone with Evan is as it always is, gentle and loving. And Evan, who cannot bear to make anyone feel bad, simply says, "That's okay, Dad. I know you had to work." Peter reaches back and pats Evan's knee before putting the car into gear and driving us home.

■ FIVE

December 2014

IT'S FOUR MONTHS LATER, a Saturday, the first weekend of December. Evan and his band, Galaxy, are performing in San Diego's Balboa Park, 1,200 acres dotted with museums, theatres, and restaurants. It is the start of December Nights, an annual two-day festival to kick off the holiday season, with vendors hawking handmade jewelry and ceramics, food trucks selling everything from tamales to cotton candy, and stages with a variety of bands and dancing troupes. The afternoon is all blue sky and gentle breeze. I lean against a tree in front of the stage, chatting with the keyboardist's mom.

Evan is the bass player and a singer in the band, a pack of four teenage boys who have been playing together since elementary school, rehearsing in their parents' garages. I remember them as little kids, their instruments bigger than they were, and now here they are, the size of men, going through their sound check with an audio engineer who works for the park. Last night the boys rehearsed in my garage, the door up and open to the warm night, a few neighbor kids hanging out in the driveway watching. I sat on the front steps of my house waiting for pizza to be delivered, sipping a Pacifico with a slice of lime floating in it. It was about as close to perfect as a Friday night could be.

Peter, also a bassist, taught Evan how to play, even though Peter plays by ear because he never learned to read music. That didn't stop him from performing with several different bands over the years. For more than a decade, Peter played with the unfortunately named cover band the Free-Range Chickens, and when I could get a babysitter I would go and see them.

That band broke up years ago, and after a couple of false starts with other ones, Peter gave up and hasn't played regularly since. He and Evan used to practice together now and then, listening to a song they both liked and picking out the bass line, note by note. But it's been a long time since that's happened; now Peter is hardly ever at home when Evan spends the night there.

Wednesday night is their night together, and Peter is supposed to pick Evan up at school after cross-country practice, which ends about five-thirty. But he has been late every week for months, sometimes two hours late, and Evan sits outside of school alone, in the dark. A few times Peter has called to tell him to walk up the road to the Mexican place and get some dinner, and that's where he picks him up. Evan will be sitting at the bar of the Super Bronco, his backpack and athletic bag on the stool next to him, eating a burrito and watching whatever sporting event is on the television, in Spanish. A few months ago, I asked Peter why he is always so late—it takes twenty-five minutes to get from his office to the school. He said it was traffic.

"I check traffic," I told him. "There is never two hours of traffic. Are you just forgetting?"

"I'm doing the best I can, Eilene," he said. That is his standard line now. He is doing the best he can. In late October, I started picking Evan up after school on Wednesdays and told Peter to get him at my house. But Peter has rarely made it; there is always a deadline he is scrambling to meet, or a late meeting, or dinner with a client. Soon Evan will have his driver's license and then he can drive himself up to his dad's. No more waiting for his father, only to get a text at eight-thirty on a Wednesday night saying something came up: "Can you just stay at Mom's?"

Even on Thanksgiving, Peter was half an hour late for dinner, claiming his GPS misdirected him. Thanksgiving is a holiday we still spend together as a family, usually at my cousin's house in Los Angeles. This year my cousin was away, so we made reservations instead at a French restaurant known for its views of downtown San Diego and the bay. The kids and I, dressed up and hungry, sat at the table for half an hour looking at menus while the maître d' stole irritated glances at us.

When Peter finally arrived, saying he had gotten lost, it didn't make sense. "There is only one Mister A's restaurant in all of San Diego County," I said. "And I texted you the street address." But Peter and Anna were already deep into perusing the menu, so Peter looked up, annoyed at me for interrupting. "Can we not talk about this now?" he asked. When the check came, Peter announced that he had also forgotten his wallet. I could not figure out what was going on with him. Was he experiencing some sort of cognitive decline or deficiency? Was he bipolar? Was he just being a selfish asshole? I never even considered that he was late because he was getting high or buying drugs or sick from the lack of them. All I knew was that nothing with him made sense anymore. Yet no matter how many questions I asked, Peter had an answer that made me feel like an idiot for asking. "I was up until three A.M. because we have a brief due today" or "I was waiting at the shop for my car and didn't see your texts" or "I was in a meeting I could not get out of and my phone was in my office" and on and on.

In hindsight, it's easy to see the signs of addiction, but in real time, it's not. I had known Peter for decades and he had always put work before everything else; his excuses felt legitimate. They felt like the truth. In the past, they *had* been the truth. Peter may have been a closeted addict, but he was also a workaholic lawyer whose sense of importance allowed him to behave in ways that hurt other people—being late, not showing up, breaking promises. And I had never known someone in the crushing grip of addiction, which can look like other things—the flu, exhaustion, depression.

Now, as the band launches into its first song, I glance back over my shoulder to see if Peter might be coming. He has missed nearly every event this year involving Evan—college counseling meetings, cross-country meets. He even left Back-to-School night early, saying he was exhausted and not feeling well. And the truth was, he hadn't looked well that night. The weather was cool and he'd forgotten his jacket, so he shivered as we walked from classroom to classroom, following Evan's schedule.

During a break, I asked, "Are you okay? Seems like you've had the flu for a long time."

"Yeah," he said. "I'm just working a lot and I'm having trouble sleeping."

"What about your weight?" I asked. "You look really thin."

"No, I'm fine," he said. "I've actually gained a few pounds in the last couple of weeks."

A couple of parents I knew at the school quietly asked me that night if Peter was sick. The next day I ran into one of them at a little market in our neighborhood, picking up groceries for dinner.

"God, he looked awful," she said.

"I know," I answered. "He's just working too much, not sleeping enough, smoking a lot."

"You sure?" she asked. "He looks like he's got cancer. Or AIDS."

The band starts its second song when I feel a tap on my shoulder. It's Peter.

"You made it," I say, relieved to see him. "You only missed the first song." He waves at Evan, who smiles back. The band plays for about forty-five minutes, and then it's time for them to pack up so the next act can get on stage. Peter gives Evan a hug. "That was great. You guys sounded really good." Evan is smiling, proud. "Thanks. Thanks for coming, Dad."

"Of course," Peter says. "I wouldn't miss it."

Evan wants to hang out with his friends for a while and get a ride home with one of their parents, so Peter and I grab his amp, guitar, microphone stand, and all his cords and walk to my car. After a few steps, Peter stops. "Hold on," he says, putting down the guitar case and the box of cords to light a cigarette. I watch as he does this, see his jeans loose around the seat and thighs, which I hadn't noticed before. He is wearing a tight long-sleeved black shirt.

"I am so tired," he says, exhaling. "I barely slept last night."

"Why?" I ask. We start walking again. "What's going on?"

"Work shit," he says, inhaling deeply. "Some really bad stuff is happening." I can feel my stomach drop—it always does this when Peter expresses uncertainty about work, which makes me fear he is about to get fired. But he's a partner, I think. He's not going to get fired.

"What's happening?" I say, not looking at him. I've got Evan's amp on a wheeled dolly and am maneuvering it around people as we walk.

"Obviously, don't say anything to anyone, because I'm not supposed to talk about this."

"*Obviously*, Peter," I say. Must he preface every work conversation with this disclaimer? You'd think he worked for the CIA. We are talking about a pharmaceutical company, one that manufactures drugs to treat things like asthma and high blood pressure, not state secrets.

"We had this big filing deadline in court, something that had to be submitted by midnight. And my team fucked up." Peter pauses to take a drag. "It was a really bad fuckup. Everything was ready to go, all we had to do was sign off and submit it, and something happened, some technical problem that wasn't even our fault—it was the court's fault—but the bottom line is we missed the deadline. And I'm the partner in charge, so it's my ass."

My mind fills with questions. Why was it his team's fault if it was a technical snafu? Why were they sending it at the very last minute? But what I ask is "Where were you?"

Peter puts his cigarette out carefully on the ground and then throws it in a nearby trash can. We are at my car and stop talking to push the backseat down and slide the music equipment inside. He looks nervous, almost frightened, and that frightens me too. Peter is always in control; he does not make mistakes and he is never weak. But he seems so fragile now, like he might cry.

"Peter?" I say, more gently. "Were you not there when this happened?"

"No, I wasn't," he says. "All the work was done, I thought it was a no-brainer. Just submit it. But some stuff happened and it wound up that it came right down to the wire. And then the technology failed and it didn't submit." The client, Peter says, is understandably furious.

"Will you get in some kind of trouble? I mean, you're a partner, and you're a human and your team is human. Is there no room for error?"

This makes Peter laugh. "No," he says, smiling. "Never. There is *never* room for error. And now there are complaints that I'm not in the office enough. I work from home—you know I work from home."

I nod. He does work from home. He did when we were married and he does now.

"They told me that if I'm not physically in the office, where everyone can see me, they don't know that I'm working. So now I go in every morning by ten, I walk around the entire floor once saying hello to anyone who is in their office, work there for a few hours, and go home. It's fucking ridiculous."

"Did you talk to Jeff about all of this?" I ask. Jeff is the head of the San Diego office; he and Peter have worked together for more than a decade. "Jeff doesn't care," Peter says. "He's got his own shit to deal with. He just wants it done; he doesn't want to have to deal with my shit too."

I'm thinking of the senior associate who works with Peter, a woman whom I know is hoping to be promoted to partner this year. I ask if that's now in question. "I don't know," Peter says. "It might be. Look, I could be fired for this."

"Really?" I say. "I mean, is this a realistic concern or are you worst-case-scenarioing it?" Although lawyers, like everyone else, are fallible, I know Peter as a very thorough and careful attorney. It seems unusual that he wouldn't have been with his team if this filing was as important as it seems to have been. Even if it was just a matter of a few mouse clicks, he has always been the kind of lawyer who would supervise those clicks, to make sure they were done exactly right. At this point, however, I don't know that Peter *isn't* the kind of lawyer he used to be.

He reaches for another cigarette. Lights it. Breathes in. Breathes out. "I don't know. I mean, it would take a lot to fire me, but it's serious. It will definitely affect my disbursement at the end of the year."

That disbursement is a lot of money, hundreds of thousands of dollars a year. I don't know how much, but I'm assuming Peter earned about $700,000 last year, although he says the firm has been stingy with salary increases. Last month he told me he needed to borrow against his draw—his monthly base salary, which adds up to $300,000 a year. Year's end is where the big money comes, when the partners spread the firm's profits among themselves, like lords of a legal fiefdom. The most senior partners and the biggest rainmakers get the most; the rest of the partners—the less senior ones—split what's left.

"Peter, I'm sure you're doing fine," I say, mostly to reassure myself.

He shakes his head no. "Not as well as you think," he says. "I haven't gotten much of an increase in the last few years." I shrug, but I'm anxious. He has built an expensive life for himself here, maybe he really is struggling somehow. He'll never be transparent about it, though. Instead he'll keep me in the dark, with my understanding that if anything happens to his job, we're all in trouble. Nine months from now, I will receive Peter's 2015 W-2 form from the firm so I can begin the arduous process of filing his 2015 taxes, along with 2012, 2013, and 2014, which he never filed. And I will learn that his gross income is exactly twice as much as I imagined. When Peter died, he was earning $1.4 million a year, although he steadfastly maintained to me—his ex-wife and someone he saw as a direct threat to that income—that he was in precarious financial straits. I will be sitting at my desk, going through mounds of paperwork needed by the IRS, and I will open the envelope from Peter's law firm, unfold the single sheet of paper bearing this number, and it will feel as if I have been slapped in the face.

I believed Peter was being honest about his financial situation, that his expenses—the mortgage for his new house, the cars, spousal and child support, college and private school tuition— were so great his salary could barely cover it all. When I learn how misled I've been, I will feel like a fool.

Right now though, standing beside my car, Peter isn't a lying millionaire but just a man who seems jittery with nervous energy, looking vulnerable. Almost weepy. I pat his back, rubbing up and down as I would a child, trying to soothe him. "It'll be okay. It will work itself out. It's a missed filing deadline," I say. "No one died, right?"

He nods, looking down at the ground. "Yeah, I know." I offer him a ride to his car but he wants to walk. "It's beautiful out," he says, squinting up at the sky. "The sun feels good—I've been inside working so much." I wave goodbye and back my car out of its spot. In the minute or two it takes me to drive toward the parking lot exit, Peter has lit another cigarette and is on a call, the phone pressed to his ear. They can't leave him alone for five minutes, I think. Five minutes, just to walk in the sunshine.

■ SIX
February 2015

TWO MONTHS LATER, AT ten o'clock on a Thursday night, Evan sits on the couch in our family room, waiting for his father to call back. Peter told him a few hours ago he wants the two of them to go to Michigan to visit Anna at school, and he wants to leave tomorrow, he thinks. Or maybe not. Peter says he is waiting to determine if he can take a few days off and says he's been trying to finish up some work at the office. It's February break at Evan's high school, or in the vernacular of the students there, "ski week," although we don't ski, so Evan would just be hanging around the house for a week.

"Do you want to text Dad and see if he got flights?" I ask. Evan is anxious, and I want to relieve that anxiety, but I can't. He doesn't know if he should pack for the trip or just go to bed. If they are going, will they leave in the morning? Later in the day? Evan wants to go to Michigan so badly that he won't reach out to Peter, because he fears pestering his father will cause him to call the whole thing off. Everything related to Peter these days is tenuous and fluid. He is the king of noncommitment.

"No, Mom, just let it be," Evan says, irritated. "He said he'll let me know." So, we wait. It's been like this since dinner, four hours of Evan sitting on the couch watching television, biting his nails, trying to avoid thinking about whether or not this trip is actually going to happen.

At ten-thirty P.M. Peter finally calls. The trip is a go and the flight is early—seven forty-five A.M.—so he is picking Evan up about six. "Thanks, Dad, I can't wait!" Evan says, and races into his room to pack.

The next morning Peter is late, and he and Evan have to run through the airport to the gate, with Peter shouting, "Hold it, hold it, we're here!" along with his last name, as the attendant starts to put a velvet rope in front of the entrance to the jetway.

When they arrive in Detroit, Peter tells Evan, almost as an aside, that he lost his wallet so cannot rent a car (he has a passport but no driver's license with him). He calls a cab to take them to Ann Arbor and then phones Anna. "Hey, can you get us a hotel room somewhere within walking distance of campus? I didn't have time to do it before I left," he says, explaining about the lost wallet and the lack of a car. Miraculously, Anna finds them a room in an expensive hotel across from campus that is usually booked. Then Peter gives Evan a credit card (which he kept in the back of his phone, not his wallet) and tells him to go hang out with his sister. I've been calling Peter to find out if they made it safely to Ann Arbor and where they are staying, but he isn't answering my texts or calls, so I reach out to Evan instead. He is at a restaurant eating dinner with Anna and a couple of her friends.

"Are you having a good time?" I ask.

"Yeah, we're having a great time," he says.

I'm under the impression that Peter just lost his wallet, not that it has actually been missing for days, and I have a photo of his driver's license somewhere on my computer. "Does Dad want me to send him the photo I have of his license? Or help him rent a car?"

No, says Evan. Dad's not even with them. "He's feeling really sick. Like he has the flu again. He started to feel bad on the plane, so he's in the room sleeping."

"Oh," I say. "That stinks. He went all the way out there to see Anna and now he's sick."

It doesn't seem out of the realm of possibilities that Peter could be suffering from the flu again. It is the middle of February, freezing in Michigan, and he has just been on a plane, a good place to catch some kind of bug. What I did not know then, in February 2015, was that withdrawal symptoms look an awful lot like the flu. Eventually, the drugs become necessary just to keep those symptoms at bay.

What Peter needed that weekend in Michigan was likely cocaine or methamphetamine—to go with the opioid pills, spoon, and syringes he no doubt brought with him—and it was probably all he could think about. I'm guessing he had done some research before leaving San Diego about how and where he could get what he needed in Ann Arbor.

Depending on the drug, where you are, and whether or not you are tapped into a network of dealers in that city, the most common way people find drugs in unfamiliar places is to go where the users go and do what they do. My guess is that Peter found the methadone clinic in Ann Arbor—on the same street, in fact, as my daughter's sorority house—and hung around outside asking people leaving the clinic if they knew where he could score what he needed. He may have asked someone lurking around a 7-Eleven store in the middle of the night or at a twenty-four-hour bowling alley, or working an overnight shift at a store, if they knew where he could get cocaine or street speed. He might have found a dealer near the university through a contact in San Diego. He may have searched on Craigslist, knowing the slang dealers use for what they peddle. One way or another, he got what he needed, because the next day when I call to see how things are going, Evan tells me Peter is feeling much better, that he rallied overnight. In fact, at that very moment, he tells me, the three of them are having lunch at Zingerman's, a legendary Jewish deli near campus, eating monstrous corned beef and pastrami sandwiches.

Evan gets home late that night. He is exhausted and goes right to bed. There are a few days left of his winter break, so the next morning he sleeps late. I am in my office working when Evan wakes up and walks in, still sleepy, and plops down on the little love seat against the wall. "Hey," I say. "So how was it?"

Evan tells me he had fun with his sister, but that Peter wound up spending most of the three-day trip in the hotel room. "Do you know what was wrong?" I ask, puzzled. "Was it a stomach flu or something like that?" I don't tell Evan that I kept texting Peter to find out what flight they were taking back to San Diego and that he didn't answer. Maybe getting sick caused him to forget to make a hotel reservation and to lose his wallet?

I am sitting in my desk chair, turned toward Evan on the love seat, who is rubbing a hand over his face. He doesn't answer. "Well, doesn't he seem to be acting weird?" I ask.

There is a long pause before Evan speaks. "Mom, this is how Dad has been acting since Anna left. This is his new normal." And he proceeds to detail for me all the crazy things that have been happening at Peter's house, things I didn't know about because my son figured this was just the way it would be, now that his sister was away at college. Peter leaving at ten or eleven at night when Evan is staying there, saying he's going up to the

Mobil station, a mile away, to get a supersize Diet Coke with lots of ice—just the way he likes it—and taking hours to return. "I usually go to bed before he gets home, but one time I was still up and he came home and said he forgot to get the soda."

That autumn, when Evan was learning to drive, his father would get into the passenger side of the Tiguan, watch Evan pull out of the driveway and fall asleep within minutes. Evan was fifteen years old, with a learner's permit, and he was driving on a five-lane freeway during rush hour with no supervision. "It was crazy," Evan tells me. "I was so nervous."

One night, very recently, Peter asked if Evan wanted to take a ride with him to that gas station convenience store to get a diet soda. He drove there in his Nissan 350Z, doing 60 MPH on a narrow side road near the beach where the speed limit is 35. "He stopped so hard, the car bounced up over the curb and he parked with one wheel on the sidewalk," Evan says. "I was like, 'Dad, what the hell?' and he said 'Oh, that's okay. That's how you're supposed to drive a sports car.'"

I'm so angry I don't know what to do. Calling Peter will accomplish nothing—he never answers the phone anymore. What was he thinking? What responsible adult behaves this way? "That is insane, Evan. That is totally unacceptable and dangerous. Why didn't you tell me any of this?"

Evan just shrugs. "What were you going to do?" he says, his face reddening, anger rising. "I stay at Dad's one night a week and every other weekend. It's not like I'm going to stop seeing him; he's my father. This is just how he is. It's been like this ever since Anna left. He just doesn't care if I'm there or not."

"That's not true," I say quickly. "Of course he cares. He's just acting like a fucking lunatic."

"I don't know," Evan says. He long ago stopped crying in front of me, but now I see a reddening around the rims of his eyes, the slight glistening of tears being held in check. "I think sometimes he just doesn't love me as much as Anna. He's not as comfortable hanging out with me."

I'm trying to figure out how I'm going to broach all of this with Peter.

"No, that's not true. Absolutely not true," I say. "Dad loves you and your sister more than anything or anyone else in the world." But I say this all the time, and it is starting to sound like bullshit, even to me, and I know it's not bullshit. He *does* love them both. But I know he can be a narcissistic, selfish jerk too. Evan isn't listening. I can tell from the way he looks that he's thinking about something else.

"Last week I was in the kitchen and Dad brought in this box from Amazon and started opening it," he says. "And he was taking out all these things you would have in a doctor's office, like cotton balls and Band-Aids and needles and alcohol pads." Peter told him he thought it would be a good idea to stock up on medical supplies, just in case they were ever needed. "I'm telling you, Mom, he's been acting so crazy I didn't even say anything about it. I just put my headphones in and told him I had to go do homework. I stayed in my room the whole night."

"What the hell?" I say. "Needed for what? The apocalypse? What is he going to get next, a gun cabinet?"

Evan smiles. "A couple of weeks ago we went to Home Depot and he got two safes. So maybe, yeah."

"Jesus Christ" is all I can say. I know Peter sometimes takes home confidential client files, and that for his own important documents and valuables he doesn't have a safe deposit box, so maybe that's why he got the safes. "You know, if you don't want to stay there, you don't have to," I add. "You can stay here." Evan nods. "Yeah, maybe I will start doing that. He probably wouldn't even notice. I don't think he even really remembers when I'm supposed to be there; sometimes he is surprised to see me."

At that moment, my instinct is to tell Evan he will *not* be staying at his Dad's again, but I don't. Peter, at least up until the last year or so, was always adamant about keeping his nights during the week with the kids. And despite the fact that Peter doesn't even seem to remember when Evan is supposed to be at his house and spends almost no time with him when he's there, that he hasn't made the boy dinner in almost a year, I still feel afraid to make that decision. When something ticks Peter off, especially lately, he can't let go of it. If he feels someone wronged him—an associate who turned in subpar work or a cashier who gave him the wrong change—he will obsess and obsess over it, getting angrier with each pass. I'm afraid of his reaction if I suggest that his behavior is endangering our son. Neither Evan nor I will defy Peter's wishes, even though Peter probably doesn't remember what those wishes are.

On top of that, Evan is confiding in me. We have an agreement that whenever we talk about his father, his sister, or his friends, it is between us—it is venting and it is confidential. That night I ask Evan if I can call Peter and talk to him about all this. I tell him I am worried and upset. But Evan reminds me of our agreement and I need him to trust me. His reports about life with his father are the only information I have about Peter now, since he has all but stopped responding to Anna and me.

After Peter died, I went over and over the conversation I had that night with Evan, asking myself why I didn't just drive up to Peter's house and demand he tell me what the hell was going on. "Why do you need sterile syringes and gauze pads? Why does it take you three hours to get a diet soda?" Maybe I shouldn't have needed to ask, maybe it should have been obvious, but it wasn't.

In my wildest dreams, I could not have imagined Peter would be using those syringes on himself, so I struggled to find some other explanation, one that fit with my notion of who he was.

Evan certainly didn't know anything about intravenous drug abuse. He was sixteen years old. He respected and admired his father, so questioning Peter's decisions and explanations—whether it was to stock up on mysteriously needed medical supplies or drive three times the speed limit—didn't occur to him.

The thing I've learned in the years since that conversation with my son is that there is no particular type of person that becomes a drug addict. People who struggle with addiction look like all of us—the lawyer in his corner office, the nurse who took care of your dying father, the mother sitting behind you at the soccer game who has been stealing painkillers from her friends' medicine cabinets.

But tonight, even though I am seeing all the signs of someone in the throes of addiction, I type "bipolar disorder" and "anorexia and bulimia in men," "cognitive decline in middle age," and "can depression and stress make someone act crazy?" into my Google search bar. I don't Google "symptoms of opioid and cocaine addiction" until after Peter dies. And that is when I will see how obvious his problem should have been to everyone, because he had so many of the symptoms: weight loss, chronic flu, sleepiness, "nodding" (falling asleep suddenly), bruises, sores, scratching. Chronic cocaine use (Peter was using that and methamphetamine, a highly addictive stimulant that affects the central nervous system) can cause ministrokes and gastrointestinal damage; it can lessen the brain's ability to solve problems, make decisions, pay attention, and remember things.

I wasn't the only person in Peter's life that didn't read these signs correctly. No one, not his family, friends, or colleagues, ever floated the suggestion that Peter might be a drug addict.

■ SEVEN

May 2015

THREE MONTHS LATER, I am in the college advising office at my son's high school, meeting with a counselor named Donna to discuss Evan's best options for college based on elaborate questionnaires he and I have completed in the last few months, as well as his test scores and projected GPA. This meeting has been on the calendar for months and, as usual, Peter is late. The counselor and I stare politely at each other and decide we'll wait a few more minutes. I try calling Peter, but it's mostly for appearances' sake, to spare my teenage son embarrassment about his father, who is no longer capable, it appears, of arriving anywhere on time. I get no answer, so I text: "Peter, the meeting was supposed to start five minutes ago. Are you coming?" No answer.

Somewhere deep down in my heart I have not given up believing Peter is the same person he was a few years ago. It's not that he wasn't an egotistical workaholic then—he was—but he made it to the important stuff. He came to Anna's college counseling meeting two years ago. He was a few minutes late, but he made it. And he texted to let me know he was "almost there, just parking, will be up in two minutes." Now, he just ignores us. I keep thinking he is going to snap out of this. Snap out of this funk, the strange sickness he can't shake, the exhaustion he can't sleep off. He still has plausible reasons for being late or not showing up. It's work, a doctor's appointment, he's still got a bad cold or it's food poisoning, the car battery is dead, there was an accident on the 805, a client called as he was leaving the office—there is no end to the explanations.

Donna, a tall, imposing woman whom I have never seen wear anything other than a dress and heels, has to meet with another set of parents in forty-five minutes. We move ahead without Peter. I text: "We're starting, so just come into the office whenever you get here."

Donna starts talking about schools she thinks would be appropriate for Evan based on his interests and academic strengths. I ask a few questions and look thoughtfully into my lap as she answers so I can surreptitiously check the time. About thirty minutes later the door opens and in walks Peter, smiling and shaking Donna's hand as if now the party can really start. He tucks his phone into the pocket of his pants and says, "I'm sorry I'm late, I had a doctor's appointment that ran over." Donna smiles her professional, closed-lipped smile. "I hope everything is okay, yes?"

He sits down to the left of me on a small sofa. "I have Hashimoto's disease," he says. "I was at the endocrinologist." I don't understand why Peter is providing these details to Donna instead of just answering yes, but I'm alarmed, so I turn toward him and ask about it. "What is that? I've never heard of it. Is it serious?"

"No," he says. "It's actually pretty common. It's a condition where your immune system attacks your thyroid, and that causes your thyroid to be underactive. Probably why I'm always tired."

"So, you went to the doctor about the lump? On your thyroid?" I ask, trying to clarify why he went to an endocrinologist, even though we are at a college counseling meeting, and that counselor is sitting right there, behind the desk, getting more irritated with us by the second. "Or because of the weight loss?" He has had a lump on his thyroid for nearly two years, but the doctor assured him it wasn't cancer, it just needed to be checked out.

"For both," he says. We turn toward Donna, outwardly calm and poised in her chair, Evan's records in her hands, waiting for Peter to finish the story of his doctor's appointment, which has absolutely nothing to do with our son's college prospects. "We only have about twenty minutes left," she says. Evan sits quietly next to me, staring down at his hands folded in his lap.

I turn toward Peter and lightly touch his knee with my fingertips, to get his attention and prevent him from glancing at his phone, which I can hear buzzing with incoming texts. "We're talking about Evan's options for college and what Donna would recommend," I say quickly, trying to catch him up on the last half-hour's conversation in one sentence and show Donna I really was paying attention. She nods politely and then picks up right where we left off. Peter asks a few questions and I turn to hear him speak, but I'm not really listening. All I can see is how awful he looks. He is so thin it is hard to imagine how his neck can support his head, and although he is wearing a dress shirt and khaki pants, he looks disheveled. Maybe it's that his face is sweaty; odd, as I am freezing in this over-air-conditioned office. I assume it's because he ran from the car to get here and it's hot out. I suddenly notice how thin the hair on his head has gotten. What remains is wispy and a little too long, so it's starting to curl at the ends. He looks like a mad scientist.

The meeting ends and we are ushered out past well-dressed parents waiting for their turn to discuss with Donna the intellectual and academic attributes of their son or daughter and the prospects for his or her future, for whom they are paying a yearly tuition that allows them to command the undivided attention of a woman who knows the insides and outs of every admissions office at every university. We say goodbye to Evan, who heads back to class. Peter looks smug as the two of us walk out and into the parking lot. Evan is smart, has great scores, will have lots of options. And he is proud of that.

Our kids attend this school because Peter wanted them to attend it. They went to our neighborhood's public elementary school—in fact, we bought the house I live in because the elementary school nearby was considered a "good one"—and Anna went to the public middle school for a year too. In fifth grade, she couldn't make sense of the math lessons, so Peter decided he would teach her fifth grade math himself. Each weeknight, no matter when he got home from work, he retaught Anna the day's math lesson, following the textbook. Some nights he whined about it, about how our taxes were paying for incompetent teachers, but once he got started he was in his element, sitting beside Anna at the kitchen table, teaching her mathematics and enjoying it. In seventh grade, however, there were fifty kids in Anna's science class and she complained that she couldn't hear the teacher or see the board. That was the last straw for Peter.

We applied for Anna and Evan to attend private school. That fall, they began the eighth and sixth grades here, at the Francis Parker School.

My car is in the school parking lot but Peter has parked a few blocks away, so he gets into mine and I drive him to his. We sit in my Prius for a few minutes first, reviewing what Donna said and what each of us thinks. But I can't just leave it at that, as if Peter isn't sitting across from me, disappearing. "You look like you're dying," I say. He starts laughing. "No, seriously, Peter, you look awful. Your skin is gray. You were sweating in Donna's office and it was freezing. And now, it's eighty degrees out and you're shivering. What's wrong? What's going on with you?"

He is still laughing. "I'm not dying, Eilene. I have Hashimoto's, I told you."

"So, is this why you've been losing weight? And why you have been sick all year? Is that what the doctor said?" I am so desperate for a reason, something that makes even a tiny bit of sense, to explain his declining health and crazy behavior.

"I guess. I have a prescription for Synthroid, so I'll get that today and start taking it. It's a synthetic version of the hormone your thyroid makes." He isn't saying what I need him to say, that once he takes this medication he'll start to feel well again. So I ask.

"And does the doctor think that once you're on that, you'll start to feel better? You'll start to gain weight and stuff?" I ask.

Peter doesn't answer, but reaches into his pocket for his phone, which has been vibrating intermittently since he got to the meeting. He glances down at it and then back up at me. "You know, the general counsel called and told me to go to a doctor. Don, the general counsel of the entire firm, called to say I needed to see a doctor."

"Really? Why?"

"I guess they were concerned about me, about my health. So he called me. And he doesn't usually call people at the firm to tell them to go to the doctor." Peter has a half-smile on his face and it is dawning on me that he is proud of this. Here I thought he was confessing something embarrassing, that he—a grown man— had to be told to go to the doctor by the management of his law firm. But no, that's not at all what this means to him. To Peter, that call confirmed his importance, confirmed how essential he is to the firm, confirmed that, yes, after all the years he has given to that place and all that he has given up for it, this firm *cares* about him. They are *worried*. And Peter is flattered by this attention, I can see that. I feel slightly nauseated sitting here, looking at the smile blooming on his large skeletal face, his teeth stained from too much coffee and diet cola, the whites of his eyes slightly yellow, jaundiced.

"Wow" is all I can say. "Do you do anything else besides take the Synthroid?" I ask.

"Yeah," he says, "I have to have another blood test in six weeks to make sure the hormone levels are right."

"Did you already make that appointment?" I ask. It's like Peter is my son, rather than my ex-husband, but it took him two years to figure out why he is feeling so bad, and I want him to get better.

"No, but I will," Peter says. I take out my phone and make a note on my calendar to ask him in three weeks if he's scheduled a blood test. "I'll remind you, okay?"

"Okay," Peter mumbles, but I've lost his attention. His head is bent over his phone as he answers a text. I start the Prius and drive around the block to where his white Nissan sports car is parked. "I'm so tired," Peter says, looking out the window toward his car, as if contemplating the amount of energy it will take to push open the door of the Prius, get out, climb into his car, and drive back up the freeway. "Maybe I'll go home and take a nap before going to the office."

"That's a good idea," I say as he closes my car door. I reach across the seat to shout out the passenger window, "Don't forget to fill your prescription!"

That afternoon I tell Evan that Peter has finally figured out what's wrong with him. "It's something called Hashimoto's disease," I say. "It screws up your thyroid. Hopefully, once he starts taking the medication for it, he'll stop sleeping all the time."

Evan starts his homework and I go online to Google Hashimoto's disease. The first thing that comes up is the Mayo Clinic website. A quick glance at it, and I can see that Peter does have many of the symptoms of Hashimoto's—fatigue and sluggishness, increased sensitivity to cold, hair loss, pale and dry skin, memory lapses, depression, muscle aches, weakness, and joint pain. I actually feel, for the first time in a long while, my anxiety lifting. But then I read that a hallmark of the disease is unexplained weight gain. Peter is the thinnest he has been in the twenty-eight years I have known him. I look it up on the National Institutes of Health website too. It gives more detail about both the gland and the disorder ("The thyroid is a small butterfly-shaped gland in the front of your neck. . . . Thyroid hormones control how your body uses energy, so they affect nearly every organ in your body. . . ."). I scroll down to "What are the symptoms of Hashimoto's disease?" They are nearly identical to the Mayo Clinic's list of symptoms, including weight gain. Every single medical website I check that night says weight gain is among the most common symptoms. I call Peter, and for once he answers. I can hear in the way his voice is clipped that he's annoyed. "Hi," he says. "I'm slammed right now, what is it?"

"I think you need to see a different endocrinologist, Peter. I looked up Hashimoto's and you're supposed to be *gaining* weight, not losing it. I think your doctor might be wrong. You should get another opinion." I know he will never get a second opinion, considering how long it took him to get the first. I'm worried though; I think he's been misdiagnosed.

"No, that is what I have," he says. "I don't know why I'm not gaining weight, but all the tests show I have Hashimoto's. So I don't know what to tell you."

"Look," I offer. "Can I find another endocrinologist that takes your insurance? I can make the appointment for you. I think you should at least talk to someone else."

"Eilene," he says, exhaling. "I just spent two hours today at the doctor dealing with this, after blood tests and all that shit. This is what I have. He's a good doctor. Let me start taking the Synthroid and we'll see how I feel. Okay? I have to go. I should be on a conference call right now."

Am I crazy? I think. Could you have all the symptoms of a disorder except one—one big one—and still have that disorder? I don't know, maybe. I get off the phone and sit there a minute, not knowing what else to do. If it's not Hashimoto's, then what? How else to explain what the last year has been like? I think about trying to find the name of the endocrinologist Peter is seeing so I can ask him these questions myself, but I'm not Peter's wife anymore and even if I was, the doctor is not going to speak to me without his permission.

Anna, now home for the summer, tells me Peter is awake at all hours of the night, walking up and down the stairs, talking on the phone, sometimes even in and out of the house. I assume it is work stress, since that was what often kept him from sleeping when we were married. There were many nights he would get out of bed and just go into the garage office to work, rather than staying awake all night worrying about getting something done the next day.

All summer, our kids have been coming back to my house early from their weekends at Peter's because he stays in his bedroom most of the time. When Anna asks him why he doesn't want to hang out with them, he says he's sick, can't seem to shake this cold he has. She has told him he needs to see a doctor, but he doesn't answer. And then there's the mouse.

He has trained a small white mouse named Snowball to respond to voice commands. Anna told me her dad even bought a book about training mice, and now sometimes takes Snowball with him to work if he is going back to the office at night. When

Peter calls to the mouse, she will climb up his arm and sit on his shoulder. He has become obsessed with her. "Evan and I were sitting on the couch just talking and Dad came in and went to pick up Snowball and play with her, like we weren't even there. It's totally weird," Anna tells me. "We just looked at each other and started laughing."

In fact, Peter and I were on the phone a few weeks ago after he returned from a last-minute trip to Florida, and he started telling me about Snowball.

"She was so pissed at me for going away," Peter said. "I called to her and she wouldn't come. She always climbs up my arm when I call her. But when I first got home she just ignored me." Peter was laughing the way he used to laugh about the funny things our children did when they were babies. That night on the phone I tried to laugh too, tried to see the humor in the mouse story, but it felt like my ex-husband was losing his mind. I asked some questions about Snowball, but what I really wanted to ask Peter was if he felt connected to reality. Ask if he was hearing voices or seeing things. Twelve or fourteen months ago, we wouldn't have been having a conversation about an angry mouse. Peter would not have made a spur-of-the-moment 3,000-mile trip to Florida without telling anyone, just to look at a vintage sports car he doesn't need. Drugs were not on my mind that night, psychosis was. Mania and borderline personality disorder and schizophrenia were. But drug addiction can look a lot like mental illness. The heavy use of drugs like cocaine and methamphetamine, especially when injected, can cause psychotic symptoms such as disorganized speech, incoherent thoughts, lethargy, and antisocial, dangerous, or erratic behavior. Long-term substance abuse can also cause what the *Diagnostic and Statistical Manual of Mental Disorders* (*DSM-5*) calls "substance-induced mental disorders," and those include delirium, depression, anxiety, and dementia.

It was not far-fetched, at that moment, to think that a mental illness like mania, combined with a lack of sleep, chronic stress, the coffee and Monster energy drinks, the sugar and fast food, the fear of slowing down, might have been the reason Peter had two car accidents in the previous month—one serious enough to take the Tiguan out of commission for at least six weeks. He was on his way home from a concert in L.A. when it happened. "It was a minor accident, I wasn't even going fast," he told me. I had wondered, though, if it was a minor accident and he hadn't been going fast, why was it going to take six weeks to repair?

The weekend after our meeting with Evan's college counselor was another one where Peter spent the entire day in his bedroom. Anna and Evan left early and drove back to my house Sunday morning. They told me Peter left his room only to walk into the kitchen to a pan of brownies he had baked. He took one from the pan and walked back into his room without saying a word to either of them. Evan would have stopped going up there months ago, but Anna continues to want to be there. She is only home for the summer and wants some time with her dad while she's here, so Evan heads up to Peter's with her, the two of them believing each weekend their dad will start feeling better and start acting more like his old self.

Monday night I call Peter to ask why he was in his room all weekend. He sounds rushed and irritated when he answers, probably wishing he hadn't. "The kids are upset," I say. "They don't understand what is going on with you. They didn't see you all weekend. What's the point of wanting them up there if you're going to ignore them?"

"I told them I was sick," he says, exhaling loudly. "I left a brochure about Hashimoto's on the counter."

"You left a brochure on the counter?" I repeat, making it a question, as if that will transform the statement into something that makes sense. "Look, if you need to rest because of this, why can't you just talk to the kids about it? They are worried, Peter. They love you."

I hear him sigh. "I love them too," he says, and then the phone is silent for several seconds. "What do you want me to do, Eilene? Tell them I'm very sick?"

I feel my stomach drop and adrenaline kick in; my heart is suddenly beating fast. I thought Hashimoto's wasn't uncommon? Wasn't serious? I lower my voice and say, gently, sensing an opening for some kind of confession, "Are you? Are you very sick Peter?" The phone is silent again for a few seconds. Oh my god, I think. It's not just Hashimoto's; it *is* something else.

"Yes," he says, more softly. "I am." He isn't at home. I know because of the noises I hear behind him, other voices, scraping chairs, music. "What do you want me to do?" he asks, not really looking for an answer, just exasperated.

I'm not sure what, exactly, I want him to do. I want him to be healthy again, but I don't know how to get him there. "If I had as much money as you do," I say, "I'd check myself into the best clinic I could find and figure out what the hell was wrong with me." At this moment, more than any other, I am so close to the truth. I am millimeters from it. One changed word—*clinic* to *rehab*—and maybe the jig would have been up, the game over. Peter would realize I had finally found the last piece of this puzzle I've been trying to solve, the one depicting a needle and a spoon and an elasticized tourniquet. But I can't locate that last piece; it's right in front of me but I can't see it. "I'm trying, Eilene," he says, finally. "I'm doing the best I can." He hangs up before I can say anything else.

Research has shown that when we are faced with evidence that doesn't fit with the way we see the world we often dismiss it, instead we cherry-pick information that supports what we do believe. This phenomenon is called confirmation bias, a psychological term, essentially, for wishful thinking. Once I formed my conclusion, that Peter was behaving oddly and losing weight because he had Hashimoto's disease, I looked for information that confirmed it and rejected anything contradictory. Even if I had known enough about drug addiction to recognize Peter's symptoms for what they were, I probably would have dismissed them because I had already decided something else was true.

Mary Forsberg Weiland, ex-wife of Scott Weiland, the front man and lead singer of the band Stone Temple Pilots who struggled with addiction, was diagnosed as bipolar at twenty-three, which appeared to fit her symptoms. At that time, she and Scott were in a relationship that eventually led to marriage. In a 2011 interview, she said her diagnosis had been based largely on her feeling "angry and jacked-up all the time." Mary blamed her arrest in 2007—for setting fire to Scott's clothes in the driveway of their home after a particularly vicious fight—on an imbalance in her bipolar medication. Yet after the couple divorced, Mary found she wasn't so jacked-up and angry anymore. In her memoir, *Fall to Pieces*, and in our conversation, she describes a pattern of mistreatment by Scott. "One day I'd be dealing with a wonderful, loving person and the next day I'm dealing with someone I don't even recognize. I didn't understand what was happening."

Mary and I talk about how easily Peter and Scott were able to spin complex webs of lies that somehow made sense, at least to each of us. Even after she and Scott divorced, he continued to lie about everything, she says, even lying about why he was in drug treatment. "I wanted to believe he was going there to get sober. But Scott went there to hide; he didn't really intend to clean up," she says. "He'd go there, get a lot of rest and attention, not have to take out the trash or watch the kids." And then he would relapse, over and over again.

"Did he make you feel like you were crazy?" I ask. Peter was certainly able to make me feel like I was, even though it was his behavior that was crazy.

"Oh my god, yes," Mary says. "Once we split up, I felt fine, I felt normal again. The doctors realized then that I had been misdiagnosed. I wasn't bipolar at all. It's that I was married to an addict."

Tonight, sitting in front of my computer, I am well into my own denial, unable or perhaps unwilling to connect the dots. I've been attempting to answer emails but am too tired, so I just put the iMac to sleep and then pull my fingers through my hair looking for loose strands, a nervous habit I have. When I look down, there is a pile of hair on my keyboard, but it's not strands I've pulled out. They are strands that have simply fallen out. "Jeez," I say out loud. "I'm so stressed, I'm losing my hair."

I turn off the lights in my office and get ready for bed. I'm under the covers reading a book when Evan walks in. He lies down across the foot of the bed and stretches, a long, full-body stretch. "Hey," I say, "It's almost eleven. Are you going to bed soon?"

Evan rolls over and props himself up on an elbow, facing me. "Yeah," he says. "I've been waiting for Dad to call—he texted an hour and a half ago saying he would call in ten minutes. I texted back and asked if he was still going to call to say good night, but he hasn't answered. I'll just text him that I'm going to bed and we can talk tomorrow. Good night, Mom," Evan says. He gets up from the bed and gives me a hug.

I watch my son, once my baby, walk down the hall to his room. He no longer has the body of a boy—it's bursting into that of a grown man. I know in another year or two he will look completely different; he will *be* completely different. Tonight, that thought makes me teary-eyed, both for what I can't have again and for what Evan doesn't have now—time with his father, which he needs. If Peter is going to call in ten minutes, what happens that he suddenly can't?

I turn off the light and feel the tears coming, so I bury my face in the pillow to keep Evan from hearing. I don't know where to turn for help or what to do. "Life can only be understood backwards," Kierkegaard wrote, "but it must be lived forwards." If only I were looking back right now.

■ EIGHT

July 8–10, 2015

IT'S TWO MONTHS LATER, eleven o'clock on a Thursday morning in July. I hear Anna come in the front door and go to her room. A few minutes later, she taps tentatively on the door that separates my office from the kitchen, in case I'm on the phone. "Can I come in?" she says softly.

I get up and open the door. "Hey," I say. She hugs me. "What time do you have to be at work?" I ask. She has a summer job at a store in a nearby mall.

"At two," she says. Her eyes are red, as if she's been crying. I offer to make her a lunch salad I know she likes, and she stands at the counter as I start assembling it. "Is something wrong?" I say. "Did you guys have a nice time with Dad last night?"

Her face collapses. In the space of ten seconds, she goes from saying "thank you for making me a salad" to an eruption of sobs, trying to talk but barely able to get the words out, shaking with the force of—what? Anger? Fear? Sadness?

"What?" I say, leaving the salad to walk around the counter and hug her. "What is it, Anna? What happened?" After a few minutes, I grab the tissue box and hand it to her. She leans against the counter across from me and blows her nose.

"Mom," she says. "This is so fucked up. Everything with Dad is completely messed up. He was so mean to Evan; he yelled at him. He was so nasty to both of us. I don't know what's going on with him, but he was being a total asshole."

She is furious. "Evan wanted to take Dad to the hospital because he was really sick. And Dad yelled at him, said that he should leave him alone, that he should stop. Evan came downstairs to my room and told me he thought we should call an ambulance. He was really upset. But what good would that do? Dad would just refuse to go. I was so pissed off about it that as soon as I got up this morning, I went for a run and then left. I didn't even say goodbye," she says. "Dad probably doesn't even realize I'm gone." We stand there, staring at the salad ingredients on the counter, and then the front door opens and closes.

Evan walks into the kitchen. As soon as he puts his keys down Anna starts crying, then she hugs him. "I felt so bad for you when Dad yelled at you last night. I'm so angry at him, I didn't even try to talk to him this morning. I just left."

I can see that Evan has no intention of crying, of breaking down the way his sister has. Something about him is hard and determined, as if his skin is thickening while we stand there. Peter's words, whatever they were, however they were shouted, hurt him, but he says nothing.

"What happened?" I say. I'm looking at Evan, but he is steely-eyed and I can't read him. Anna steps away and wipes her eyes, then answers for him, telling me that she and her brother had gone to get some dinner because Peter was sleeping and there was nothing to eat in the house. When they returned, Peter was awake. He walked into the kitchen looking very sick. "And then he started going off on us, just yelling at us, and it didn't even make sense," Anna says, looking at Evan. "Right?"

"Yeah," Evan says. "Dad started yelling about people at work that are driving him crazy, just complaining about everyone and everything."

He continues. "I went into his bedroom afterward to make sure he was okay and he was sitting at the edge of his bed not saying anything. All of a sudden, he just bends over and throws up. I don't know what it could have been because he hadn't eaten while we were there. But it was dark, almost black, and thick. And then he just threw a washcloth down over it. So I said, 'Dad, I am calling an ambulance. I'm taking you to the hospital' and he started shouting at me. He said, 'No! Leave me alone!' and then he said, 'You're just like your mother. She's always nagging me to see a doctor and that's what is making me sick.'"

I am silent although my mind is going through a kind of triage reasoning. Black vomit, sleepiness, irrational anger . . . those are symptoms of . . . what? Vomiting is not a symptom of Hashimoto's. So what does it signify?

I don't yet know the vomit is something called hematemesis, blood that has been exposed to the stomach's acid, causing it to thicken and darken. It's often described as resembling coffee grounds. Doctors at Emory University School of Medicine in Atlanta describe it in the textbook *Clinical Methods* as a sign of "acute intestinal bleeding, usually from the upper gastrointestinal tract." With hematemesis, the loss of blood can be substantial.

"In one small study," the doctors wrote, "all six patients with hematemesis had lost more than a quarter of their red cell volume." The most serious complication of this kind of hemorrhage is tissue hypoxemia, which is what happens when the body's tissues aren't getting enough oxygen (delivered to them by blood).

The human body can tolerate up to about a 15 percent loss of blood volume, but if it continues, the person hemorrhaging will start to get thirsty and feel faint. According to the textbook, when blood loss hits 40–50 percent, a "complete loss of the ability to compensate occurs with shock, impaired flow of blood to vital organs, tissue hypoxemia, lactic acidosis, and ultimately, death." Peter had always suffered from gastrointestinal problems—he ate Tums as if they were candy. Opioid and amphetamine abuse makes stomach problems much worse. But I don't know any of this yet. All I know is that last night Peter vomited something dark and thick. And he yelled at Evan, to whom he has rarely raised his voice.

"Then," my son continues, "when Dad walked back to his room I shouted down the hall 'I am only doing this because I love you.'" Anna starts to cry again. I feel tears burning on the inside of my own eyes, but force them back.

"Did Dad say anything else?" I ask.

"He yelled back, 'I know, I love you too.'"

I put my head in my hands. I do not know what to do with this information. Go up there myself and confront him? Call the police to check on him? And with my luck, they will bang the door down, walk in, and he'll be eating lunch. Peter will call me as soon as they leave and read me the riot act. *"You called the fucking police? Because I have Hashimoto's? Because the kids aren't getting enough attention from me? Are you fucking insane?"*

Anna walks away from Evan to get a tissue and leans against the counter, her hands folded across her chest. "It's like . . ." she says, crying, and the words sound like she's wrestling each one of them out. "It's like he doesn't love us anymore." I put my arms around her.

"No," I protest. "Don't say that. He loves you guys more than anything else in the world." Maybe I'm not very convincing because I'm not convinced myself. *Does he?* He used to, but what about now? If he loved them and wanted them at his house, why is he ignoring them? Why is he shutting them out?

"No, Mom." Anna wriggles away from me. "He *doesn't*. You don't know, you're not there. You don't see how he's acting."

Evan is standing in the family room, a step down from the kitchen, tossing a small green ball up in the air and catching it, over and over again. "Evan," I say and he stops.

He is wearing a blue T-shirt with the words *Waffle House* printed over a photo of a waffle, a Buffalo Bills cap on his head. He turns to face me.

"She's right," he says. "That is exactly what it's like."

ANNA AND I SPEND all of the next day trying to reach Peter. We need to make arrangements for the weekend, find out if he's feeling better and figure out what to do about his car. His Tiguan was supposed to be Anna's to use this summer, but it's been undergoing repairs from the accident he had in late April; it is ready to be picked up today. We can't do that without him and he's not responding. (A month from now, with $1,000 still owed for repairs, the car will be repossessed by the San Diego County Credit Union.) I leave a message on Peter's work phone about all this, hoping his secretary will hear it and track him down.

After dinner, frustrated and angry and worried, I decide to go for a hike in Mission Trails Park to clear my head. It's only a few miles from my house but it feels rural and far away, 7,000 acres of rugged hills, open valleys, even a couple of small mountains. It's so quiet here but also so alive, with the sounds of birdsong, of squirrels, mice, and snakes rustling in the brush, of crickets starting their chirping as the sun goes down. The mountains ahead of me are pink, and in the sky, thin strings of clouds lit from behind glow orange, crimson, and lavender.

As I walk, I struggle with my conscience. We have not been able to reach Peter in two days. This has happened before, but not when he was as sick as he is now. I am both worried about him and afraid of him at the same time, and have been vacillating all day between driving up to his house and forcing him to go to the emergency room and not doing anything, just waiting it out.

Years later, when I think back about that night, I will recognize that I knew in my heart some kind of crash was coming. I didn't understand why it was coming or what it would look like when it arrived, but I knew it was inevitable. And soon. It seemed impossible to me that Peter would be able to continue to function much longer—personally and professionally—while so sick and distracted, vomiting, sleeping much of the day and then being irrational when he was awake.

I know one reason I didn't drive up that night and try to drag him to the ER was because I was sure he would not go, would fight with me the same as he did with Evan, and I would leave questioning myself—my logic, my sanity. I felt sure that if I just waited a little longer the inevitable crash or breakdown—whatever it was going to be—would finally occur. I believed the end of this madness would be a trip to the hospital for Peter, and with that a proper diagnosis and treatment plan for whatever was wrong. And then his and all of our lives would start to make sense again. I never considered he might die. Peter had become so powerful, so busy, so depended upon by clients and co-workers and family that it felt to me—and likely to Peter—that he was *incapable* of dying. This was a man who went to work the day after he had a motorcycle accident that fractured his elbow and scraped off a good deal of the skin on his arms and legs. Only the weak-willed took sick days, in Peter's estimation. He never did.

It's dark when I get back to my car, the air thick with the smell of sage, evening primrose, and jasmine. Stars litter the sky. I open the door and ease myself behind the steering wheel.

Tomorrow morning, I decide, no matter what, I'm driving to Peter's house and taking him to the hospital. I'll call an ambulance if I have to, but he's going. Enough is enough.

PART II

■ NINE

July 11, 2015

I'M OUTSIDE PETER'S HOUSE, standing in the street, the phone pressed against my ear, the 911 operator my lifeline, the only thing keeping me tethered to the here and now. I'm sobbing, gulping air, saying to her, "Are they coming? Are they on their way?" She reassures me the ambulance is on its way. Then I hear the sirens. "Okay," I tell her. "I can hear them. Can you wait until I can see them?" Yes, she answers, she can stay on the phone with me as long as I need. Two minutes later, there is a fire truck, an ambulance, and two police cars are outside Peter's house.

The first people to reach me are EMTs, both of them young men, their faces blank and experienced. Used to this. "Can you tell us what happened?" the taller one asks. I unload in a torrent of details and tears what I've discovered. "I tried to do CPR," I tell them in my nonstop narrative. "The 911 operator told me I should try, but I couldn't move his arm. I don't think you can move his arm, it's very stiff." The men keep nodding at me, as if nothing I could say would ever surprise them. "Thank you," says the tall one. "We'll go in and see what we can do." I nod. I'm so cold. It's eighty degrees outside, and I am shivering, my teeth chattering.

I retreat to the backyard and a policewoman enters with a male partner behind her. Her name is May. She asks me some of the same questions as the EMT guy.

Anna texts me—she's about to leave for work—"How's Dad?" I look at my phone and look at May. "My daughter is asking about her dad. I . . . I . . . do I tell her?" There is nothing that can prepare a mother to tell her children their father has died.

May puts her hand over mine, in an effort to dissuade me from any impulse texting. She suggests instead that I tell them only to come up to their dad's house. "That way, when you tell them," May says, "you will have the grief counselors here to help." About five minutes after the police arrived, two women, grief counselors who volunteer for the police department, walked gingerly through the open back gate. They are both retired nurses who spent decades in hospital emergency rooms. These are women who know unexpected death and the hysterical disbelief that surrounds it, and they know it well. I text Anna back "Can you guys come up here? Drive carefully, there's no rush. The ambulance is here. They are working on Dad." Anna texts back in all caps "WHAT DO YOU MEAN WORKING ON DAD? IS DAD OKAY?" I don't want to lie, but I don't want to tell the truth. "They are with him right now. I'll know more when you get here. Don't rush. It's fine. They'll be here for a while."

About twenty minutes later my kids arrive. Anna charges through the open gate into the backyard, Evan behind her, staring at his sister's back. She looks around with wild eyes and I can see her physically beginning to panic, taking in the police and firefighters and the two EMTs going in and out of the house. "Mom," she says, glancing around. "Mom! Where's Dad? Where's Dad?"

Her voice is shrill. Evan is silent, his downcast eyes are unfocused, staring at a point somewhere behind me. He is afraid, I think. He is afraid of what's coming because he knows what's coming. He was the last one to see Peter alive.

"Mom!" Anna yells at me, her eyes still darting around the yard. The grief counselors are behind me, standing with sympathetic looks on their placid faces. They aren't stupid, my kids. They know something horrible has been set in motion, they just need me to say the words. And I do. I walk toward them and I am shaking as I take my daughter's hand. "Daddy," I say, pausing for a millisecond. "Daddy died." I say it again, as my kids stand there looking at me. "He died." Anna yanks her hand away and covers her ears. I start crying. "I'm so sorry," I say, sensing that in a moment, all hell is going to break loose. "I'm so, so sorry." Anna looks at me as if I'm crazy. "What?" she shrieks. "What are you saying?" And then "No, No. No. What the fuck! WHAT THE FUCK? Dad died? No, no, he can't be dead. No!" She is screaming.

My son puts his hands on his head and starts sobbing, the way he hasn't cried—big choking sobs—since he was a little kid. His face is beet red. Then it's like he's gone blind, or his head is too heavy to hold up any longer. He puts both hands out in front of him, trying to feel his way to the ground, as he crumples onto the grass.

"Anna," he shouts, trying to interrupt her shrieks, "can we just lie down?" He yells it louder. "Can we just lie down here for a minute?" His arms are reaching up and out to her. She turns to look at him and stops screaming, as if she just remembered he was there too. And she does lie down in the grass, she and her brother holding each other and crying. I know they feel guilty for not getting Peter to the hospital. I feel guilty, too, and probably more than they do, since I'm an adult and I could have done it.

The thought of him so sick that he had to lie down in his under-wear and socks on the bathroom floor, had to put his head on an empty box, that he was unable to sit up or to dial anyone's number for help, even 911, just three buttons, that he might have been in terrible pain or just afraid and alone, is making me want to pull my hair out.

On my drive up to his house this morning, I mentally steeled myself for what I'd find—I figured he might be sleeping or even, potentially, semiconscious. I would call an ambulance. His bed might be covered in vomit or urine. I readied myself for all of that. I'd even brought a book with me, preparing for what could be a long wait in the emergency room. And I said out loud, as my stomach began to shake and the rest of my body started to feel cold and shivery, "It's not like he's dead. He's not going to be dead or anything." My hands were sweaty on the steering wheel.

Now I am bent toward my sobbing children, unable to move. I want to lie down, too, onto the neglected green-brown grass. I want to shimmy right in between my kids and be cocooned and hidden, not be the person everyone is looking to for directions and answers and assistance. I have been shaking from shock and fear almost continuously for three hours, and I am so tired I could probably sleep standing up. Instead I crouch down in a squat and put my head in my hands and pull myself together.

Anna and Evan are, after all, just teenagers. It's been more than a year since Peter acted like any kind of parent, and they need to believe I have things under control, that I know what I'm doing. When Peter and I split up five years earlier I fell apart, and for two months spent most of my time in bed, crying. Ever since then, any time I get teary-eyed, Anna will put her hand on me and say in an urgent voice: "No, Mommy, don't be sad. Don't be sad. Don't start crying again." I need to hold it together now.

I stand up. It feels like I'm in the middle of a slow-motion hurricane, my life literally coming apart at the seams. Everything around me is washed out in the noon sunshine and heat, a slight breeze making the thicket of wind chimes hanging over the porch of the house next door bang together, creating a tinkly, dreamy, dripping-water sound. Everyone is standing and waiting for the sobbing and screaming to die down, for the kids to sit up, for the mom to say something. The grief counselors have pamphlets in their hands, the police officers and the medical examiner cling to their clipboards and pens. There is information that has to be gathered for the death certificate, for the police report, for the autopsy, before they can go home to their own, presumably intact, alive families, and chalk this up to another day's hard work.

Then my daughter disengages from her brother and starts walking toward the house while rapid-fire texting, holding her phone directly in front of her face, screaming and crying the whole time. She nearly bowls over the grief counselors trying to be of service. She stops, looks at them, and then looks back at me. "What the fuck are they doing here?" she screams. I explain that these are counselors here to help us. I want Anna and Evan to sit down and talk to these calm women, who appear to be completely unmoved by any of the hysterics taking place around them. But Anna is behaving almost as if she's been violated. To me, the backyard containing all this medical and police activity feels like a crime scene. To her, however, this is an intensely private event that has turned, by all appearances, into some sort of vulgar circus.

Out of the corner of my eye I see Evan, red-faced, sobbing, weeding the gray and white gravel path, picking out the tiny green plants that try and poke through to the sunlight. Peter kept asking him to do this, saying he would pay Evan $10 an hour to weed the gravel, and he did do it, sporadically, but he hated it and recently flat-out refused. Evan knew Peter was just giving him something to do instead of spending time with him—which Peter couldn't physically do, at that point, because he was either out of the house or sleeping most of the time. Now, wracked with guilt and remorse, Evan is crouching down, picking out every green leaf and blade of grass he can find.

One of the lawyers with whom Peter works, the head of the San Diego office, is walking into the backyard. He is saying a neighbor called him, someone who had seen all the commotion in front of Peter's house. But what neighbor? And why would they call Peter's boss? I'm confused but don't have time to ask these questions because the cops are looking at me for approval: Do I know this man? I don't immediately recognize him, so he says, "Eilene, it's Jeff. Peter's partner." And then I remember: Jeff. Peter's boss really, as well as his colleague, for many years. To the extent that lawyers at this level in the firm's hierarchy have any friends at the office, Jeff was one of Peter's.

A few minutes later, Evan, Anna, Jeff, the grief counselors, and I are in the house's first-floor bedroom, which was Anna's before this morning but is now a waiting room for everyone other than emergency personnel. The police and EMT people are upstairs in Peter's bedroom, taking photos and clearing out drugs and syringes I don't yet know exist, documenting everything they see and wrapping Peter's body in a pale yellow bag in which he will be transported to the morgue. May and the other police officer are filling out paperwork on the white counter upstairs in the kitchen. None of us in the downstairs bedroom want to see Peter's body being brought down—even covered by a bag—so we're hiding out instead in this hot room, the sun pounding on the other side of the closed room-darkening curtains.

Anna is kinetic with grief and anger and cannot sit still. She's texting her friends and walking around the room in circles. I wish Jeff would leave. I'm not sure why he feels the need to be here, witnessing all this. Twenty minutes ago, after I remembered who he was, I started shouting at him. I hadn't realized until I saw him how angry I was with the law firm where they both work; how angry I am with Jeff, the other partners, the clients, all of them.

"That job killed him," I say, crying, raising my voice. "You guys and all that pressure and the clients always coming first." Jeff doesn't say anything, doesn't try to defend himself or the firm. Everyone working at Peter's level in Big Law is working just like he was, with that same intensity, and they aren't all dropping dead from it.

We sit for a minute, not saying anything. "He hadn't even really showed up the last three months . . . really the last six months," Jeff says quietly. What? I'm thinking. No, no, no. He was working all the time, that's why we could never reach him. That's what he told us. The client breathing down his throat. The complaints about his attendance because he was working from home. Surely Jeff knows that, right?

The medical examiner—her name is Angela—is sitting beside me. We moved outside to the patio as soon as Peter's body was taken from the house, so we could talk away from Anna and Evan. Angela is a young woman with kind eyes and a very gentle manner. This is a person who is accustomed to seeing all kinds of death—from homicides to motorcycle accidents to suicides to heart attacks, which at this point is what I'm assuming has taken Peter's life. She asks me questions about that morning, almost exactly what the police asked me a few hours earlier. Then she asks me about Peter's history. Any mental illness I knew about? Any drug use? Any problems with alcohol? It seems an odd line of questioning until I remember the bloodied hole below Peter's elbow.

"Wait a minute," I say. "Are you asking me these questions

because of that hole I saw, the one that was bleeding, below his elbow?" Angela nods once, an almost imperceptible up-and-down with her head. There is a clipboard on her lap, and I can see into the bag next to her. It's filled with papers. She has a photo ID in plastic on a lanyard around her neck. Angela is so patient, just sitting there, waiting for me to catch up to her.

If you could crack open that particular second or two in time and examine what was happening in my head, here is what you would see: I have a picture in my mind of Peter's arm, pale, skinnier than I have ever seen it, but still, just his arm. And there, oddly, is what I assumed to be some kind of cut, some small injury that may have happened as he fell. If he fell. Or before he lay down on the floor to rest. To have the heart attack I am assuming he had.

The little injury was caked with dried blood. Or maybe not exactly dried, but not new. Not red. Not red enough to have alarmed me, so it had to be old and darkened by time. The only thing that struck me as odd, though, was that it seemed so round. Like a little puncture. And then there was Angela's nod. One nod, on the heels of those questions about alcohol and drugs.

And now, in an instant, I know what she is trying to tell me: that it is a self-inflicted injury, or not really an injury at all. Indeed, it *is* a hole. In that split second, I know what she's thinking. And I want to laugh at how wrong she is, how mistaken her line of thought. It's completely ludicrous. "No," I say, shaking my head. Now we understand each other. "No way." He was a lawyer and had been a scientist, a chemist, someone who knew exactly the kind of damage a particular compound or drug could do to the human body. "He . . . he . . ." I'm struggling to articulate all that is going through my head at that moment. "He went to Cornell. He . . . he is rich." Angela nods again. "He lives . . . he lives here. In Del Mar. This house cost two million dollars."

She has a look of such compassion for me at that moment, it's suddenly clear I'm the ridiculous one. I'm defending Peter. And I'm admitting that without even consciously knowing it, I have completely bought into the stereotype of a drug addict—poor, living in a squalid apartment with other addicts, or homeless under a bridge, or sitting at an intersection off the freeway with a cardboard sign that says *Homeless veteran. Anything will help*. Not a white, wealthy, well-educated partner in a prestigious law firm. That is definitely *not* what an addict looks like.

"I know," Angela says. "We actually see a lot of this now. Wealthy, high-powered executives that overdose and die, usually from some combination of amphetamines, opioids, and other drugs. I think Peter probably died of an overdose. We won't know until the autopsy, but that's what it looks like."

Wait, what . . . an autopsy? My mind is racing. Why? Why do they need an autopsy? I didn't ask for an autopsy. And anyway, he died from working too hard, isn't that clear?

"But . . ." I am searching for anything, anything that will make what Angela believes is true not be true. Because in my mind it *cannot* be true. It would be like telling me the sun doesn't, actually, rise in the east and set in the west. That it's the exact opposite— rising in the west and setting in the east. We are talking about a man that used to snap at me for using my teeth to open stubborn toothpaste caps. Calling it stupid, to risk cracking a tooth. How does a man that gets pissed off about the irresponsible use of teeth to open toothpaste caps inject things into his body? Into his veins?

"But," I say, starting to cry, "he had kids. We have kids. They were here, they lived here part of the time." Can't she see how crazy what she's suggesting would be? Angela nods her sympathetic nod. Anna and Evan are still in the downstairs bedroom, talking to the grief counselors. Well, Evan is talking to the grief counselors. Anna is texting and crying and pacing.

"Are you sure?" I say. "How do you know?"

"There were injection marks on his arms and legs," Angela says.

I'm stunned. I was standing over his prone body, I was yelling into his face, shaking his shoulders. I touched his arms, pulled at the right one, trying to move it aside so I could do chest compressions. I didn't see anything at all. Except that one bloody hole.

"I didn't see injection marks," I say softly, bewildered. A few months later, when I'm doing a special kind of therapy called EMDR (eye movement desensitization and reprocessing) for post-traumatic stress disorder, I will learn that when faced with extreme shock or anxiety, it's not uncommon for the brain to develop a kind of tunnel vision. Overwhelmed by an event, the brain decides to see only what it needs to see. And in this case, it saw a body on the floor. My brain decided everything else was superfluous.

Angela turns her body so it is angled slightly toward mine. "What do you think it was?" I ask her. "Heroin?"

"I think it was probably amphetamines," she answers. "Cocaine. Maybe other substances too. But again, that's why we'll do the autopsy, so we can determine the cause of death."

I don't even really know what an autopsy is, other than observing the occasional forensic pathologist character in movies and television shows. "There were marks all over?" I ask again. It's like I'll have to hear it a hundred times before I can get my head around it, believe it.

"Yes," Angela says. "On his torso too. And the police collected a lot of drugs and drug paraphernalia—there were safes with pills, baggies containing a white powder, syringes . . ." She's still talking, but the voice in my own head is louder.

Where were these syringes? These safes, where were they?

Why did they take them without asking me first? Powder? I didn't see any powder. I'm so confused and yet, as horrible as this information is, it's also a relief. A bigger relief than I ever imagined.

Everything suddenly makes sense. And no sense. Peter was a drug addict. *Of course* Peter was a drug addict. The whole country is in the throes of an opioid crisis, and he had all the symptoms. My mind is running roughshod over this new information, scrambling to keep up, to process it. No wonder he was acting the way he was, illogical, undependable, nonsensical, dangerous. Now I get it; I get all of it. Why he had to leave abruptly that morning last summer in Michigan, the weekend we took Anna to college for the first time. Why he missed the football game. Why he fell asleep on the furniture in the Ann Arbor Target. Now I see why he lost his wallet a hundred times, why he was twenty-five minutes from Evan's school but took two hours to get there. Why he seemed to have the flu for months. The weight loss. The brittle hair and yellowing teeth. The shivering when it was seventy-five degrees outside. The never wearing short sleeves. What an idiot I am. How clueless and naïve and racist and classist. I thought I knew Peter so well, this friend and former husband and co-parent and sometime-nemesis that has been a part of my life almost every day for the last twenty-eight years. But I didn't. I missed it— who he was, whom he had become—a deception so deep it feels obscene.

Jeff is still here, he's been sitting in a chair listening this whole time, but now begins speaking to Angela, the medical examiner. In her report from that afternoon, she wrote, "The decedent's boss reported that around November 2014, the decedent's work had started to decline. He was missing calls from clients and failing to show for appointments. This was really unusual behavior as the decedent had previously been one of his top attorneys and an extremely hard worker." Jeff also tells Angela that a co-worker had seen a package of tourniquets delivered to Peter's office. This she will also include in her written report.

Now I have to decide if I should tell the truth to my children. I look at Angela. "Do you have kids?" I ask. I wish Jeff would leave. I don't want him privy to this, but I don't know how to say that.

Angela looks surprised. "Yes," she says quietly, not in the habit of talking about herself in situations like this.

"What do you think I should do?" I say. I'm feeling desperate for someone to just make a decision for me. "Should I tell my kids the truth?"

A grief counselor has silently entered the patio area and is beside me now, as if she knew I'd need her. Her presence is ethereal, calm, supportive. I fantasize about asking her to come live with us for a while, but instead give her an imploring look. "What would you do?"

Angela and this retired nurse exchange a glance. After a few moments, Angela says, "I would tell them the truth." The grief counselor agrees. "They are going to blame themselves for not getting their father to the hospital, especially your son, because he saw him last." In fact, after I told Evan and his sister that their father was dead, the first thing he said was, "Oh my god, I should have taken him to the hospital. I should have taken him to the hospital," and then he collapsed, sobbing, onto the lawn. Evan had tried to take Peter to the hospital, but when you're sixteen and your father yells "No, leave me alone!" you back off. Even if your father is vomiting. Even if he's mumbling incoherently most of the time. Or falling asleep upright in a kitchen chair while reading the mail.

Angela says, "I think the truth will be very freeing for them. They will understand there was nothing they could have done."

"Okay," I say. I believe in telling the truth, I always have. The truth is important, is liberating, is healthy. If nothing else, every-thing will finally make sense. They can stop guessing about what was wrong with Dad. So I finish the paperwork with Angela, and then we call the kids out to the patio.

I ask Anna to put down the phone, that we have something important to tell them. She does. She's so angry and frantic right now I can feel the heat coming off her body, like she wants to jump out of her seat and hit someone.

"It looks like Dad died of a drug overdose. He was a drug ad-dict. He has needle marks all over his arms and legs. So there was nothing any of us could do, because he kept it a secret from all of us. That's why"—I turn to Evan—"he wouldn't go to the emer-gency room. He didn't want anyone to know."

Anna is ashen. "A drug addict? How? Why?"

I have no answer. "I don't know. I am as astonished as you are. But it makes sense now, all the weird stuff he was doing, the car accidents, the long, nonsensical texts. The big rant he went on Wednesday night."

Anna nods. Her anger is dissipating. "Yeah, it totally makes sense."

Evan is visibly, physically relieved, almost instantly. It was as if his whole body, inside and out, had been clenched like a fist for the past two hours. "Well," he says, "that puts the whole thing in a different perspective. Now I understand, it wasn't our fault. So there really was nothing I could do about it, right?" He is looking at Angela and the grief counselor, but especially the counselor, with whom, I now see, he has been talking about this very thing, what he could have done. It's the conversation we will have with one another over and over again in the coming months, the one that tries to answer the question: Could we have saved Peter?

Evan's entire being is pleading with us to say the words he needs to hear, and the retired nurse does. "No, there really was nothing you could do. I mean that." The other grief counselor is here now too, and this one glances at her counterpart. "We both worked in the ER for many years and saw many, many addicts overdose and die. There is absolutely no way you could have stopped this. It wasn't within your power." Evan nods his head up and down, breathes out. I can see that until this moment, he's blamed himself entirely for Peter's death, for not insisting his sister help him force their father to go to the emergency room.

"Okay," he says. "I just need to know I couldn't have saved him if I had gotten him to the hospital that night." Both Angela and the nurses are shaking their heads, saying no. "When someone is addicted, there is very little you can do to help them, truly," one of the counselors says. "The only person that can help an addict is the addict. If they don't want to get help, you can try all you want, but you will not be able to save them."

This was the right thing to do, I think to myself. They are calmer. I'm calmer. All this mounting craziness is over, and it finally makes sense. If nothing else, the not understanding-anything that was going on—and the anxiety that created—has now come to an end. I'm not yet sure what this information, this truth, will bring any of us, other than the spreading warmth of relief I feel at this moment. But there is something incredibly powerful about it.

After I sign the required paperwork to take a body to the city morgue and have it autopsied, and the grief counselors (how they do this for free, I still can't fathom) provide me with a list of places that perform cremations, as well as the requisite "What to Do After Someone Dies" pamphlet, and Angela gives me a list of companies that will clean up death—disinfecting the floor where fluids have leaked and the dying have soiled themselves—and Jeff tells me he will connect me with "the folks in HR" Monday to deal with questions of salary and health benefits and life insurance, my kids get into their car and I climb back into mine. Anna keeps asking me if I am okay to drive. The police ask too.

What is "okay to drive" anyway? How many times did Peter drive our son when he was high? How many times did he shoot up in his bedroom, with Evan and Anna sleeping just down the hall? I'm not intoxicated or medicated, I'm in shock. My brain is shutting out all the horrible things I've seen so I can't quite re-member seeing them, but it's not shutting down generally. I can certainly see the road, understand the traffic patterns. And the last thing in the world I want right now is to be with other people. I want to be alone; in fact, I *need* to be alone. Five hours in the company of EMTs and cops and grief counselors and Peter's boss, having to repeat what I saw and what I did over and over again, every single step I took recounted to the emergency responders and police and then the medical examiner and my kids. All I want is to sit in silence.

My daughter is driving right behind me, in the car that be-longs to her brother now that she is at college. They are tailing very close behind me, so close I can see they are talking; my daughter now desperately afraid I will be the one to die next.

I feel just the way I did when Peter and I first separated six years ago, like I'm under water, every movement slow and heavy. Back then I couldn't imagine how I would make it without Peter, and that's what I'm thinking again, now, as I merge onto the 805 South. I'm not sure how to be in the world if Peter isn't in it too. For the last twenty-five years I've measured myself against his expectations, living my life in partnership with—and in opposi-tion to—him, always seeing myself through his eyes and then making adjustments to get him to see me the way I wanted to be seen, although it never happened. Even in the first few hours of this new, post-Peter world, I am acutely aware of my lost bear-ings.

My legs feel heavy as I drive, and I am bone-tired. As I round the corner to my street, I can see some of my friends getting out of cars with food in their arms, making their way toward my house. Jennifer and William, who live a few blocks away, look as if they are carrying a boatload of bagels and cream cheese. Irina is balancing a pan of roast chicken in her arms, and her husband, Gary, carries what I assume is a tureen of soup. Joan and her husband, Steve, and Bette and Edit, and Sabine, some of their children too, all of them are walking up the front steps of my house. This is my family. I have told just two people that Peter died, no more information than that, but here are ten people, about to carry whole dinners and plates of cookies and bottles of wine into my kitchen, which they know well. I sit in the car a minute before getting out. I know this is the end of one kind of misery and the beginning of another. No more of Peter's manic, crazy, hurtful, frightening behavior. Now, instead, I will have to navigate a continent of grief and anger and shock. I will have to be the widow, even if I am no longer the wife.

THE FRONT DOOR IS open to the street the whole night, with people coming in and out, eating, drinking, speaking softly and urgently, teary-eyed. When the night ends, I won't even remember seeing people clean up, but the dishwasher will be running and the dining room and kitchen will look as if no one had been there.

Several of Anna's high school friends, now college students, are in the living room with her, hugging. They have, for some odd reason, brought water balloons and Silly String—the kind of string that is shot out of a can. It occurs to me that teenagers don't know the first thing about death etiquette. Water balloons? Silly String? That's what you bring to cheer up a friend whose boyfriend ditched her, not what you bring when someone's father has just died. On the other hand, they are providing comfort to Anna right now and that's what she needs. A friend says to me, "You should sit down. Have you eaten? Eat something." I will, I say, but first, I head down the hall to Evan's room. I knock. "It's me, honey, it's Mom. Can I come in, please? Evan?" There's no answer, so I open the door and walk in.

Evan is lying in bed, earbuds in. He's just staring up at the ceiling, not looking at anything. He sees me and takes out the earbuds. I climb into his twin bed and put an arm around him. "Did you hear Simone and Katie knocking? They want to come in and see you. Can they?" I can see his eyes are bloodshot and red-rimmed. His hair is a little sweaty and matted. I put my chin on his head and inhale deeply. My sweet boy.

"I can't, Mom," he says. "Is that really bad? I just can't right now. I don't want to talk to anyone." We lie there together a minute, and then Evan rolls over onto his side.

No, I tell him, you don't have to see anyone if you don't want to. "Can I bring you in some food or something? Water? Juice?" But I know that all he wants is to lie here and try to fall asleep and wake up and have it be Saturday all over again, a regular old Saturday. No dead father. No drugs, no police. No stiff bodies covered in yellow tarp being carried downstairs. On this let's-try-it-again Saturday, Evan will wake up, work in the garage music studio we created in his dad's old office, and then he'll drive up to Solana Beach with his bandmates and go to the Bro-Am, a charity concert and surf competition where one of his favorite bands is headlining. It'll be beautiful there and he'll come back sunburned and happy, hair smelling like salt air. I stare at his back, his earbuds in his hands, and I know he is waiting for me to leave so he can plug in again and shut out the world.

■ TEN

July 12, 2015

IT'S BEEN BARELY ONE full day since I discovered Peter's body, and now the kids and I are heading up to his house to clear out anything of value to us—real or sentimental. A friend's sister, who is a lawyer, urged me to do this, reminding me that Peter had been hanging out with drug dealers who are just now learning he is dead. I don't know if they will try and get into the house, or if any of them has a key.

I ask my friend and neighbor William to accompany us. I know the house will be exactly as it was yesterday, only Peter's body will be missing. Everything else, the pandemonium of the master bedroom, the stains on the bathroom floor, the drugs the police didn't find, the vomit, the bloody sheets—everything will still be there, waiting to be cleared out and cleaned up. It's too frightening right now to go alone.

To William, the house is just walls and windows and doors and rooms. To us, it feels like a living, breathing, monstrous thing, harboring all sorts of secrets we have yet to uncover, truths we don't know. Anna and Evan are anxious and sad in the car on the way up to Peter's house, and I am also anxious, but not sad. I won't feel sad for a long time. I have to get past angry first, and I am very angry. I am enraged at Peter for dying like this, for being so stupid and arrogant, for his drug use and his selfishness.

The closer we get to the house, the quieter it is in the car. I can smell the ocean. There is a buzzing in my stomach and head as I take the Carmel Valley Road exit off the freeway and turn left at the light, heading west. My heart is racing like it's yesterday all over again, except I can see William's white Honda behind me. We drive past cars parked on the side of the road that leads to the state beach, boogie boards sticking out of back windows, parents helping young children into swim trunks and flip-flops. I make a right onto Peter's road, climb the hill, and then pull into the driveway. William parks his car on the street. Anna, Evan, and I sit in the driveway a minute, looking up at the house, summoning our collective courage to open the car doors and get out. It's hard for me to believe that less than twenty-four hours ago, Peter was here and this place was a hive of police and EMT activity. It's quiet now, surreally peaceful. Birds in a bird feeder, a lemon tree heavy with fruit near the back fence.

All at once we're out of our cars and walking to the side gate. Evan plugs in the security code and we walk through the yard to the glass front door. I open it and feel a rush of cool air that smells like yesterday. My legs shake a little as I walk upstairs, the kids and William behind me, into the kitchen. "What's that smell?" Anna asks, crinkling her nose. She opens the fridge. It is the smell of sour milk and rotten fruit and spilled condiments. "Ugh." She closes it. I notice there's some water on the floor. "Looks like it's leaking," I say, and open the refrigerator door again. Half-empty wine bottles crowd the glass shelves, along with jars of jam, Nutella, a bag of chocolates, soda, Vitaminwater, energy drinks, milk. It looks like the refrigerator of an alcoholic with a raging sweet tooth. The fruit in the produce drawer is covered in fluffy white mold and the contents of what was once a bag of spring-mix lettuce has begun to liquefy. How long has it been here? How long had it been since Peter ate real food?

The freezer doesn't seem to be working right either. It looks like it hasn't been defrosted in decades, although it's probably not even five years old. Ice is everywhere it shouldn't be, several inches thick, and embedded in it are bags of frozen peas, micro-waveable dinners, veggie patties, and ice cream—so much ice cream. "Let's not open it for now," I tell Anna, who is standing next to me, also peering into the freezer. "I'll have to clean it out and get someone to fix it." The list of things I will have to do in the next few months to get this house ready for sale feels insurmountable.

I have brought boxes and bags into which we can load items we want to take today. Anna wants to go start in the master bedroom, but I don't want her to see the bathroom floor, which I know is stained with blood and feces and vomit and urine, all in the vague outline of her father's body. But she is becoming frantic to get in there, to get as close to Peter as she can, so William says he will go in first to remove anything—mostly drugs but also, possibly, sex-related paraphernalia—she shouldn't see. I start to walk in with him but my body thinks Peter is in there, and for the first time in my life I know what it means to have your knees buckle. It's as if my kneecaps change from a solid to a liquid, the rubbery tendons and ligaments bowing outward. I don't fall as much as I crumple down. "Mom! Mom!" Anna screams, thinking I am fainting. "I'm okay, I'm okay," I say. But I don't go into the bedroom.

William systematically combs through drawers in the dresser, in the closet, in the bathroom, in the night tables. He looks under the bed, and checks all the shelves, depositing things I can't see into a cardboard box. Then he tells Anna it is okay to come in. She races to Peter's dresser, which sits below a window overlooking the backyard. Before I left yesterday, I pulled down the shades so that the neighbors—with a back porch that allows a clear view into this bedroom—can't see the disaster in here. From my perch in the hallway I can see both the dresser and Anna. She is pulling shirts off the floor and out of drawers, putting each one to her face and inhaling to see which shirts still retain the smell of her father. Those are the precious ones, the ones she is jamming into empty bags and boxes. She buries her head in each piece of clothing, grabbing at anything Peter might have worn or touched. She wants everything, dirty or clean, on the floor, in the hamper, lying in a heap under the bed—she wants all of it, every scrap. She's like a starving person, desperate for whatever crumbs were left behind.

Evan is in the living room and kitchen, wandering around, opening cabinets and drawers as if seeing the house and its contents clearly for the first time. Anna tells him to come in and grab some clothes. "No, that's okay. Just take what you want," he says loudly from the living room. But Anna insists. "No, Evan, come in and take some things for yourself. You are going to want to keep some of this." Evan ignores her—he is not going in there—so she grabs a few T-shirts for him. I already know he'll never wear any of it, that it will sit in a drawer or a box somewhere because it can't be thrown out, but it can't be worn either.

William emerges with boxes full of things like expensive stereo speakers, notebooks, cameras, all kinds of electrical and USB cords, an iPad, and Peter's work bag. Inside the bag is $1,000 in cash, a pill bottle with no label, and an Advil bottle—both bottles contain a variety of different colored and shaped pills. There are three slim silver tubes of scar cream, individually packaged alcohol wipes, and tiny clear plastic tubes I have never seen before. Later I will learn they are plastic needle caps, presumably from hypodermic needles that were used at the office. William has taken Peter's iPhone and wallet off the bed and put them in the bag as well. There is a small spiral notebook with what looks like notations about daily injection times and dosages of tramadol (an opioid painkiller in the same category as morphine) and cocaine, a combination usually referred to as a "speedball." Tramadol works to lessen pain by attaching to certain receptors in the brain, which changes the brain's perception of the pain. It also allows the chemical messengers serotonin, which makes us feel good, and norepinephrine, which makes us feel energetic and alert, to hang around the brain for a longer-than-usual period of time.

Peter was able to organize himself to get drugs, but not anything else. All of this is sandwiched within a thick stack of work-related papers and a yellow legal pad with notes about client matters scrawled unintelligibly in blue ink.

A week from now, I will use the thousand dollars to pay American Cremation Service to transfer Peter's autopsied body from the city morgue, cremate it ($595 before tax), and get me a permit to spread the ashes in the ocean. I will use what's left to purchase two small pewter urns, one for each child. In hindsight, I will wish I had purchased urns for Peter's parents and siblings, but I didn't have time to think it through—the city had autopsied the body and wanted me to do something with it; they wouldn't hold it there for long. Peter's death was so unexpected and shocking that my concerns at first were all about helping my kids deal with their trauma and grief. But very soon I learn that death comes with a host of very pragmatic, non-lofty concerns. How much does it cost per day to store a person's bodily remains in the morgue? How much does an autopsy cost? How will I get the remains to the crematorium? Where can we legally spread ashes? Will the crematorium put some of the ashes in each urn, or will I have to do it? How heavy will the ashes in the box be—will I be able to carry it into the house by myself?

I will spend months repairing and emptying out Peter's house, cleaning out cabinets, drawers, closets, shelves, laundry room, garage. The number of things he accumulated over the past five years is staggering.

There will be stuff everywhere and a good deal of it random, like a shopping bag full of never-used wrapping paper rolls and birthday cards, foam surfboards (Peter didn't surf), a silver measuring tool for pasta, and a beautiful salt bowl from Williams Sonoma. In the kitchen cabinets, I will find high-end baking pans, some with price tags still glued to their surfaces, three different kinds of olive oil, two different kinds of salt, craft beers, craft root beer, cases of organic, Stevia-sweetened craft sodas, two coffeemakers, boxes of new CDs, many of them in duplicate. Discarded receipts will be stuffed into every nook and cranny, most from CVS Pharmacy. All Peter ever seemed to buy there were prescriptions, medical supplies, and candy. Lots of candy.

Long after Peter's house has been sold, I'll learn that craving sweets is a common side effect of opioid abuse. Opiates relieve pain by acting through what are known as mu-opioid receptors in the brain, and that has an effect on sugar intake and regulation of the body's blood sugar levels. Clinical studies have shown that opiate use often produces a preference for sugary foods, and researchers speculate that's because sweet-tasting foods activate the body's own pain-relieving system. Sugar, it turns out, may actually enhance the experience of the opiate user. Even if sugar hinders the effects of opiates, as some other studies have shown, it still results in greater cravings—both for sugar and for drugs.

In the bathroom cabinet in Peter's bedroom, I will find several unused enemas, perhaps needed for the chronic constipation that comes with opioid abuse (there is actually a term for it, *opioid-induced constipation*), discarded needle tips, cotton balls, scar cream, rubbing alcohol, Band-Aids of all sizes, and two gigantic bottles of tramadol from Mexico, which the police missed. There is a roll of what I think is toilet paper—it will actually be a relief to see something so ordinary in a bathroom—until I try to use it and realize, when it will not tear, that it isn't toilet paper at all. It is a roll of latex tourniquet.

On the bedroom floor I will discover a large cardboard box from Patrick James, a high-end men's clothier in town, which contains more than a thousand dollars' worth of clothing Peter ordered the previous February. He hadn't even opened it. In the back of his closet I will find a stack of shoeboxes taller than I am. On the outside of each box he has taped a photo of the running shoes inside. Another shoebox will be found behind the washing machine, only this one won't have shoes in it. Instead it will contain a square mirror, its surface still sticky with a filmy white residue, a tiny glass tube, a multicolored headband Peter must have used as a tourniquet, an actual rubber tourniquet, syringes, loose pills, tweezers, and two small baggies with milky quartz pebbles I will later learn are crystal methamphetamine. Perched on the shelf in Peter's night table I will see a cashier's check dated June 1 from Citibank for $4,492, written out to an auto body shop he has already paid. On the receipt from the bank that day I will note an additional withdrawal of $9,950 in cash.

The garage, however, will be the worst, like a multilayered time capsule with boxes buried under boxes holding all the detritus of Peter's life, from childhood, his twenties, our marriage, and after marriage, a period in which he purchased a lot of things that probably seemed like good ideas at the time (or a good idea while high) and then turned out not to be. There will be an unopened Sonos Playbar system worth close to a thousand dollars, although the house already has one, three bicycles, and two new televisions still in their boxes. I will work my way through crates of old record albums, several sets of speakers, guitars, unwanted furniture, unwanted window treatments, tool sets, motorcycle gear, car washing and waxing kits, unopened kitchenware, big bags of Halloween candy. A metal cabinet against the wall by the water heater will hold enough medical supplies to open an urgent care clinic, as well as pills, lighters, and more of those little glass tubes, which I will learn are used for smoking meth. There will be a tower of Vitaminwater Zero variety packs from Costco, cases of protein bars, storage bins filled only with power cords and surge protectors, old computer keyboards and monitors, window screens, a new Blu-ray DVD player, shelving that hadn't been unwrapped, two grills, and on and on it will go.

At the bottom of all this, its top partially crushed inward, will be a box that holds evidence of who Peter had been long ago, when I first met him. Inside will be his business cards from Adam Personnel in New York City, his Eagle Scout patch, a silver charm with a Native American–style design strung on a leather necklace, some photos of him playing bass at a bar in Syracuse, a photo of the two of us in our tiny cottage in upstate New York, an old passport.

Although that box had been forsaken long ago—carried around from place to place only because it hurt too much to toss it—going through all the old things I remembered will break my heart. This was the man I'd fallen for back then.

I will be both archaeologist and anthropologist, combing through the physical evidence of this man's life, preserving the ordinary and unremarkable, things like grocery lists, hastily written notes to the kids, receipts, silly photos, a children's piano book with which he once tried to teach himself piano, his favorite coffee mug. In death, these objects have been transformed; now they are history. Every scrap of paper with Peter's handwriting on it is an irreplaceable artifact. The last cup from which he drank can never be washed. The last guitar pick his fingers held, the needle tip that may have penetrated his skin before he discarded it onto the bedroom floor—are saved. Even the stain in the bathroom made by his prone body will feel sacred; as do the discolored sheets, the sticky residue on the night tables; the pill bottles with their psychedelic handmade labels.

It will become my job to create a true and meaningful history of Peter through these objects, all of which I will package up and transport to a rented space in a self-storage facility not far from my house.

Anna, meanwhile, will curate her own private stash of items, salvaged when she was alone at Peter's house. She will keep them in a sturdy cardboard box—one she will name "my most precious and important things"—on a shelf in her closet. After she goes back to school in September I will peek into it so I can understand better whatever is in her head.

There will be a sheaf of papers on which Peter had made lots of work-related notes, specked with spilled coffee and stained with ink from his fingers. There will be little notes he wrote to Anna and her brother and left on the kitchen counter, telling them he was out on a run or working but would be back later. There will be an expired passport and an old driver's license, nearly every medal for every race Peter ever ran, a collection of recipes the two of them often used to make dinner (back when Peter still cooked meals). Her box will also contain some loose pills she no doubt found in her father's bedroom, an asthma inhaler, a half-used tube of face cream, even two loose Marlboro cigarettes. Peter's hands had pulled them out of their box at some point and put them—where? In a jacket pocket? A pants pocket?

In the glove box of his car? Perhaps between his lips for a second? And they somehow wound up rolling around a kitchen drawer. I found them while cleaning out the kitchen and meant to throw them out but never got to it. When I see them in Anna's box, their creases tenderly smoothed out, their delicate paper bodies lying like little mummies in a protected corner, my heart will hurt.

She also saved a few of the slim notebooks in which her father had recorded injection times and dosages—and which addiction psychologist Sam Ball, head of the executive treatment program at Silver Hill Hospital in New Canaan, Connecticut, says shows Peter had almost surely lost control of his drug use. "His choice about using was probably gone the moment he felt he needed to keep monitoring it, felt the need to have some kind of system, to keep it from getting any worse," Ball told me.

Evan will save some things too—a coin collection of Peter's, the old driver's license, a corporate ID from when he worked in pharma, and a couple of pairs of earrings. What means the most to him, though, are Peter's bass guitars, record albums, and CDs. Evan will probably come to know his father by listening to the same music Peter did, some of it at the same age Peter was when he first discovered it. Evan will also save his father's used guitar picks. One of those tiny purple plastic picks, worn down in the middle from Peter's thumb, Evan will put in his wallet so he can have it with him all the time. In September, I will take it to a jewelry maker in San Diego who will create a silver holder for it engraved with Peter's initials. Evan will wear it like a dog tag, every day, on a silver chain around his neck.

When he leaves for college later this year, I will find a plastic grocery bag holding a forgotten pair of pants and a favorite T-shirt, way back on a shelf in his closet. I will wash them and pack them up to send to Evan at school, first calling to let him know I found them. "You don't have to send those," he will say. "They are . . ." I will hear him hesitate. "They are the clothes I was wearing that day." He'll pause. "At Dad's house."

"Oh. okay. Well, they're clean now," I'll say with a laugh, trying to make the moment less heavy. "I'll just put them in storage, okay?"

"Yeah," he'll say. "That would be perfect."

The word *storage* is really the word *limbo*. It's the place for all the things no one really wants, at least not yet, but that can't be thrown out either. There these things will stay for however many years is enough time for Anna and Evan to be ready to confront them. The plastic bag with the clothes Evan was wearing on the worst day of his life will become part of this collection, but there won't be room for most of everything else in Peter's house, the majority of it unimportant to his children anyway. It is hard to imagine that it gave Peter any kind of lasting happiness, and research actually shows it doesn't. Studies done by consumer psychologist Marsha Richins, a professor at the University of Missouri, found that although people who like to buy things feel happiness at the moment of purchase, it doesn't last. "Research consistently shows that high-materialism consumers are less happy than others," she writes. We adapt pretty quickly to more, bigger, and better, she says. People who are less materialistic likely find emotional fulfillment elsewhere, suggests Richins, through pleasurable experiences, interpersonal relationships, spirituality, and other intangibles.

Peter was addicted to more than just drugs; he was addicted to work, to shopping, to sugar, to status, to power, to money. The experience of each of these hit the pleasure center of his brain, pinging or flooding it with dopamine. But he was also trying to figure out what "success" looked like and how it felt. Did it look like a house with an ocean view? Like fifteen pairs of running shoes? Did it feel like a $3,000 mattress? Robert H. Frank, an economics professor at Cornell University and author of the book *Luxury Fever,* says when people at the top of socioeconomic and professional ladders need to answer the question "How am I doing?" they look at those around them. "All competition is local," he says, "so the answer to that question is very flexible. As you get higher up on the ladder you have a much higher level of opponent." In Peter's case, the opponents were the attorneys with whom he worked, sending their children to expensive private schools, driving their new Porsches and BMW sedans into the firm's parking lot.

Juliet Schor, a sociologist at Boston College and author of *The Overspent American* and *Plentitude: The New Economics of True Wealth,* says for those at the top—financially and socially—it's not just about consumption but about conspicuous consumption. "The more money you can waste, the more you can show how wealthy you are," she says. "Society has naturalized insatiable desire, the idea that you can never have enough."

SEVERAL WEEKS AFTER WILLIAM helps us take the first load of valuables from Peter's house, I will receive a copy of the autopsy report; a couple of months after that, the police report; and a year later, police photos taken at Peter's house after I called 911. Together these represent a terrifying and remarkable accounting of his death and, in an odd way, his life too. The autopsy report reads like a cross between a true crime novel and a grocery list, with a detailed accounting of the physical body, the weight and condition of each organ, of blood vessels, of bones and skin.

It starts with a cold, clinical description of Peter's physical body, "a well-developed, thin, Caucasian man" and "the body measures 73 inches in length, weighs 170 pounds." It becomes an unemotional commentary of what is normal and abnormal in a human body. Peter is mostly normal—symmetrical facial features, symmetrical ears, lips that are free of trauma, teeth that are "natural and in fair repair," facial hair consisting of "irregularly shaven whiskers in a usual distribution," and so on. It's also a story, the ending of which reads: "Cause of death: infective endocarditis due to injection drug abuse."

Peter did not overdose. Instead, he contracted an infection that became the "infective endocarditis" listed under "Cause of Death." Bacteria entered his bloodstream through one (or more) of the tiny injection holes in his body and seeded itself in his heart (most likely in its valves) and from there it multiplied exponentially, traveling into his kidneys, liver, spleen, and brain. He likely died from some combination of infection and heart failure. According to the attached toxicology report, Peter's blood tested positive for benzoylecgonine, hydrocodone, and dihydrocodeine. Cocaine abuse is usually confirmed by the presence of benzoylecgonine, a compound that is formed when the liver metabolizes cocaine. Hydrocodone is an opioid pain medication, and dihydrocodeine is also an opioid painkiller (frequently compounded with aspirin, acetaminophen, or caffeine), similar in structure to codeine. It's often used in cough medicine.

"The upper extremities are normally formed," the autopsy report continues. "There are prominent needle tracks with multiple punctures, ecchymosis (bruising), and scabbed blood on both upper extremities." The report notes Peter's tattoo, a "sun-type design on the left lateral arm. There is a horizontal, 1-½ inch, linear scar in the right lower quadrant of the abdomen. There is a 3-inch needle track along the distal lateral right forearm, vertically oriented, with gray scarring and numerous punctate scabs and surrounding yellow-green ecchymosis."

I remember the night he got that tattoo. A guy named Guf did it, in Ocean Beach at Ace Tattoo, which was located above a Mexican restaurant. We went to a bar beforehand and both of us, a little drunk, decided Peter should get a tattoo. He consulted with Guf about what the tattoo should look like—a sun of some sort, but with an edge. They settled on a sun with whirling blades in the center, something I never really understood but that Peter loved.

The scar on Peter's abdomen tells another story, of his emergency appendectomy at seven, after a nighttime of intense pain—so intense Peter told me he could remember sweating and shivering—but, for some reason, he didn't leave the bedroom to tell his parents. He felt that he might get in trouble for not staying in his bed. In the morning, they rushed him to the hospital. He started suffering in silence early, it seems.

The next section of the report focuses on the internal exam. This is the substance of an autopsy, where each organ is inventoried—examined, weighed, and then described. "The right lung weighs 820 grams and the left weighs 770 grams."

"The duodenum, small intestine and colon are unremarkable."

"The gallbladder mucosa shows a typical velvety green appearance. The bile ducts are patent and of normal caliber." It's both beautiful and profane.

Near the end is the "Microscopic Examination" subsection, where slivers of tissue from the vital organs are examined for evidence of disease or infection. This is the story of risks taken, vulnerability, and neglect. Here in black and white is the extent of Peter's endocarditis, a listing of the many organs in which bacteria had infiltrated and colonized, where it had flourished and, ultimately, triumphed.

The police report is shorter than the autopsy and has different details, focused more on the scene at Peter's house than on his physical condition; it's less grocery list, more true crime. What the report and photos have in common is how little of what they chronicle I remember; so many details about Peter and the house I still cannot recollect.

The police call Peter "the decedent" or "the victim," as in "the male victim was wearing only a pair of red underwear and a pair of black socks on his feet." Why "victim"? I wonder. A victim of what? "The victim had several minor wounds on his body . . . and bruise marks throughout his body." I was right up against Peter's chest, listening for a nonexistent heartbeat, I was holding his arm, and yet I didn't see any bruising, nothing unusual except that one hole by his elbow.

I decide to look at the police photos. The way they were taken, it's like walking into the house all over again on July 11. The front yard, the entranceway, the backyard, the stairs, the kitchen, the hallway, the door to the bedroom, the bloody sheets, all of it. I can smell the dry grass, yellowed and brittle in the heat. There is Peter's white sports car parked on the street, the windows so dirty you can't see inside. I forgot about the lights strung across the patio, leftover, I imagine, from some past night of merriment.

There are photos of Peter's body from different angles as well as close-ups of his arms and legs. It's impossibly difficult to look at these, but I want to see what I didn't see. Every time I pull one of these photos up on my computer's screen I have to walk away for a few seconds with my hands over my eyes. Then I walk back, peering through my fingers as if I'm watching a horror movie until I find the courage to remove my hands and take in the entire image. The details my mind shut out are here now, in full color, on my computer screen. Here is a six-foot-tall Peter (who, five years earlier, was twenty pounds overweight), so thin his knees and the knuckles on his hands seem to be proportioned wrongly, the outline of his ribs so clear it's as if he is holding his breath.

Peter's head is far too big for his neck; right below I can see his collarbone, protruding and elegant, like a woman's.

The police report's description of his arms and legs is brought to life in close-up photos that reveal an otherworldly galaxy of black and red pinprick stars scattered among blue and purple clouds of bruising. I study the police report, trying to take it all in. I'm trying, illogically, to figure out the timing of Peter's death. I don't know if it was actually that morning. I want to know what happened and when. I want to know if I could have saved him.

If I had come up that Friday morning—instead of Saturday morning—could I have prevented this? Despite what the medical examiner and the grief counselors said, the futility of this inquiry isn't obvious to me, not yet anyway. I'm still haunted by the what-ifs. No matter how useless this line of questioning, I feel compelled to ask.

I call the doctor named on the autopsy report—Steven Chapman, deputy medical examiner—and ask him if there was something different I could have done, something that might have saved Peter's life. Something besides what I didn't do, which was recognize his drug addiction.

Dr. Chapman is kind to me. "Everyone wants to know that," he says. "Could they have done something to save their loved one?" Peter, the doctor tells me, was extremely sick, his vital organs in the choke hold of a virulent infection and shutting down. A piece of the aortic valve in his heart had actually broken off. There were colonies of toxic bacteria ("septic emboli," the autopsy report calls them) all over his heart, in his kidneys, liver, spleen, and brain. Dr. Chapman said Peter's brain showed evidence of bleeding, which may explain the irrational thinking and the tirade he directed at our kids two nights before he died. And he was weak and sick from his drug habit. I take all this as a kind of confirmation of what we've already been told—that none of us had the power to save him. And what would we have saved him from, anyway? Peter, if he had lived through the night, would have needed heart surgery, weeks or months of antibiotic treatment, and even if he somehow, miraculously, recovered, the statistics say he would likely have gone back to using drugs four times before ever getting clean.

"It was noted that the body still had warmth to it and was in a state of rigor mortis," reads the report. Rigor mortis is the stiffening that happens to a body after death because of the loss of adenosine triphosphate, or ATP, a molecule that carries energy to living tissue and gives muscles their flexibility. Rigor mortis generally starts about two to four hours after someone dies. The small muscles stiffen first—the ones in the face, neck, arms, and shoulder—and then the larger ones, with the whole process peaking twelve to twenty-four hours after death. Peter's small muscles were already stiff when I got there—his face was in a kind of half-grimace, which I thought meant he'd been in pain when he died, but it was simply his facial muscles contracting. I will never know what Peter was thinking—*if* he was thinking, or if he was anesthetized by the emptied syringe on the edge of the bathroom sink—as he lay dying. No amount of physical evidence will ever tell me that.

If a body is warm but stiff, the time since death is estimated at three to eight hours. Peter's body fit that description. Yet there is this small detail in the police report: "I noticed that there was a light on in the victim's bedroom. No light appeared to be needed during the daylight hours." Those are the least clinical sentences in the report and also what makes them the most heartbreaking. He turned on the lamp beside the bed. At some point on Friday night, Peter turned on the light, like anybody might do when getting ready for bed. He was able to do that. He was still alive. But by morning, he wasn't.

For months, I go over and over the police report, until I begin to see that it doesn't really matter if Peter died at midnight or at three A.M. or at nine A.M. Because no matter what I think might have happened if I had done something different, I didn't, and I can't do anything different now. So yes, he was able to turn on his beside lamp that Friday night. He was also, somehow, able to load up two syringes with a light brown concoction of what was probably cocaine and tramadol, and carefully set them on the edge of the bathroom sink. It troubles me that I only know they were there because I can see them—one empty, one full—up close in the police photos. I was crouching right below that sink the morning I found Peter, but I never saw the syringes.

There is so much I didn't see, or didn't want to see.

The mess of the house. Cleaning supplies and books and baby wipes and toilet paper all thrown haphazardly onto a side cabinet in the hallway. The night tables in the bedroom cluttered with half-drunk bottles of diet soda and Vitaminwater and dirty drinking glasses. Beats brand in-ear headphones, a cigarette lighter, portable hard drive, writing pad, and a syringe, empty except for a reddish-brown substance caked at its tip.

On the floor beside the bed are socks, khaki pants, black jeans, and piles of other clothing. There are open legal-size envelopes, their contents extracted, lying on the floor; packages strewn about, some opened and others not. More piles of clothes against the door and a stand-up mirror; on the floor an empty box of cigarettes, pieces of torn paper, and a washcloth covering the bloody vomit I know is there because Evan told me about it. (The police have also curled the washcloth back to show the camera.) On top of that washcloth is another cigarette lighter and a bloodied tissue, beside that, an unused, still-wrapped Band-Aid. There are two digital alarm clocks, one on the night table and one on the floor. The one on the floor reads "12:50 P.M."—about eighty minutes after I called 911 for help. On the side of the bed is a 7-Eleven Big Gulp soda that's two-thirds empty, an orange straw poking out of the lid and an empty Vitaminwater bottle next to it. There's a small yellow-lined pad tucked behind the bed pillow, which Peter was using to record injections and dosage. On the bed, atop the rumpled and blood-spotted white sheets, I can see a red tourniquet, Peter's iPhone, the card key for his office, and his wallet.

The bathroom looks as if it's been ransacked, like a crime scene. The framed map that used to hang on the wall is leaning against the shower, and there are the remnants of egg cartons, cardboard toilet paper rolls, and boxes scattered everywhere. These were the building blocks of a homemade habitat Peter had created for Snowball, his pet mouse (which was found dead under the bathroom sink). Had he dragged it into the bathroom so Snowball could keep him company? Did he destroy it because he was angry? Frantically looking for something? Was he lonely? Scared? In pain? But if that was the case, why didn't he call someone? His phone was right on the bed. Around the broken mouse habitat are cotton balls, pill bottles, caps from pill bottles. There is a small wooden stool in front of the sleek bathtub.

On that stool is a yellow and green plastic box that presumably held drug paraphernalia. Next to it, a silver garbage can, missing its lid, and inside, bloody tissues. On the sink I can see Peter's razor. Was he actually able to stand up and shave? There's even a washcloth next to it, which he would have run under hot water and pressed to his face to soften the bristly growth before applying shave cream. The floor is filthy, a yellowish-brown liquid staining it.

In one photo you can see the police photographer's torso reflected in the bathroom mirror, like a bad dating-profile selfie. I zoom in on a shelf beneath the mirror and see a lighter, an almost-empty glass bottle of Diet Coke, a syringe on the shelf, empty but used. A bottle of Synthroid—the only prescribed drug in the room—for Peter's thyroid condition. Farther down the shelf is another lighter, an asthma inhaler, a half-used tube of Neosporin, and a pair of reading glasses.

On the sink sit several plastic boxes, including an oblong container for flexible "dry fit" bandages, several boxes of "tough strips" bandages, and more tubes of Neosporin antibiotic cream. In the boxes are syringes—they appear unused but unwrapped—and cotton pads, rubber bands, plastic caps, and what look like miniature silver bowls for heating things, along with a tiny scale. In another box, more Band-Aids, sterile syringes, a University of Michigan shot glass. There are toilet paper rolls sitting on top of what looks like a silver letter opener. I'm trying to understand why there are so many toilet paper rolls and how they are used in this ritual. There's lavender-scented hand soap in an Anthropologie-esque bottle and skin cream for shaving (a rare glimpse of what normal life once looked like), a small silver spoon with an orange plastic handle bent at the neck (so the spoon part angles up), a very small red plastic bowl over which is poised a syringe, empty but used.

The other syringe on the sink, next to the red bowl, is filled and ready to go. There is a Sonos system speaker, its top dusted with the white, pebbly powder of crushed pills, a gray haircomb, a big white rock of some sort, and a Ziploc bag with white powder in it. Behind all this, on the walls and on the sink, is the splatter of bloody vomit.

BY THE TIME I am able to walk into Peter's bedroom again, a few weeks after his death, professional cleaners have mopped up fluids and wiped down walls and cabinets and cleaned off the sticky residue that seemed to cover every surface in that room. They have thrown out all the garbage, folded clothes, made the bed.

A couple of years later, when I'm still doing EMDR therapy, I'll start to see—in my mind—other things I didn't remember, a few vague, flashing images. The dead mouse in the bathroom, the little cuts around Peter's fingernails, the words *Hugo Boss* on the waistband of his briefs. I will be sitting on a small sofa in my therapist's office, and in front of me, held up by the kind of stand that holds sheet music, will be what looks like a very small blackboard. In the center of the board is a small circle of green light that can move back and forth horizontally. It reminds me of the Lite-Brite game I played as a kid. My therapist, Kim, will sit to the left of the board holding a remote that controls the speed of the little green light, and can activate or halt its movement. Some EMDR therapists use a light bar instead of a light screen, others use handheld devices that vibrate back and forth between a person's two hands. I knew of one therapist who asked clients to simply tap their fingers rapidly back and forth on alternating thighs. The common denominator in all of this is bilateral, or two-sided, movement.

Before watching the light, Kim and I decide on a painful memory or thought I want to target. For months after I first start this treatment, I just want to get the image of Peter's dead body out of my head. EMDR will make those memories less visceral and more like something I might have dreamed than something that actually happened. After Kim and I decide on a memory, I will bring it to mind and then try to describe how it feels, in my body, to be thinking about it. The tightness in my chest, the feeling that I'm about to cry, the churning in my stomach, the shortness of breath. It might seem an odd way for a therapist to treat someone with traumatic memories—asking them how their *body* feels—

but there is a great deal of research that shows a strong connection between emotions and bodily sensations.

The green light begins to move back and forth across the screen as fast as my eyes can follow, and I think about how my body feels as I remember. I find that the more agitated I am, the faster I want the light to move. Often I feel a buzzing of anxiety rising up in my chest, around my eyes, getting more intense and then gradually dropping off. Images that are related and sometimes completely unrelated will pop into my head. After a minute or so, Kim will stop the light and ask, "What came up for you?" After I explain what I saw and what I am feeling, she will say, "Okay, go with that," and I will continue to follow the light.

For reasons that are not well understood but that seem to be connected to what happens to our brains during REM (rapid eye movement) sleep—when our eyes move rapidly from side to side and we dream—this kind of therapy allows associations to arise and, for me at least, both the memory and its corresponding feelings are transformed. The intensely frightening and disturbing memories of Peter's death and the months leading up to it, the condition of his house, the drugs I found there, my fear—all become softer, more muted, less intrusive. EMDR allows me to process my traumatic memories and, somehow, helps me feel better, both my mind and body. I can sleep without seeing Peter's face the minute I close my eyes. I can lie down on my mat at the end of a yoga class with my arm bent at the elbow and resting on my abdomen—the way Peter's arm was positioned when I found him—and not have a panic attack.

In his book, *The Body Keeps Score*, psychiatrist Bessel van der Kolk wrote that "knowing *what* we feel is the first step to knowing *why* we feel that way." In 2007, van der Kolk and several colleagues published the results of a study they conducted that compared the effectiveness of different treatments for trauma. Patients received either EMDR, the antidepressant Prozac, or a placebo. After eight EMDR sessions one in four patients were completely cured (their PTSD scores had dropped to negligible levels), compared to one in ten for those taking Prozac. Van der Kolk reported that eight months later, 60 percent of those who had received EMDR still scored as completely cured; all those who had taken Prozac relapsed when they went off the drug.

During one session soon after I view the police photos, the phrase that sums up my state of mind is "I am powerless." It's the feeling that I don't have control over anything, because if I did, how could this have happened? How is it this was able to happen right in front of me without my seeing it? In the year and a half or so before Peter died, I had found every possible reason for his erratic behavior and declining health other than the most obvious—that he was a drug addict. Stress, exhaustion, mental fatigue, poor diet, depression, bipolar disorder—all of those I considered. That he could be an IV drug abuser? That never occurred to me.

Was it my own implicit biases? Was it intentional? In the same way my brain narrowed my vision that morning in July when I found Peter on the bathroom floor, deciding for me what I could psychologically and emotionally handle, did I unconsciously or, on some level consciously, narrow my understanding of what was happening? And if I did, was that because I felt I didn't have the power to do anything about it? Felt I did not have the power to get Peter to admit he needed help?

EMDR also allows for the "installation" of positive feelings and associations; for that, the green light moves very slowly. Near the end of this session, Kim will ask me to describe how I *want* to feel, rather than how I'm actually feeling. The phrase I will be working toward believing is: *I cannot control everything, but I am not powerless.* It will take a while, but I will come to understand—really, deeply understand—something that should have been obvious: *I cannot control anyone else's choices.* As powerful as addiction is, there was a period of time—and perhaps that period was so small and the window so narrow that if you blinked you would have missed it—where Peter was not yet battling an addiction. He was just having what he considered a good time, hanging out with other people who liked getting high. But he made choices during that period, conscious choices, to keep going, to kick things up notch by notch until he was putting needles into his veins.

Whenever it was that Peter crossed that line from consciously making decisions to just responding to his addiction, it was also a point at which none of us who cared about him could have exerted any control. Nothing I could have done, nothing our children could have done, would have changed that. Something else was at play then, something I don't understand and Peter probably didn't either.

■ ELEVEN

July 23, 2015

IT'S BEEN TWELVE DAYS since Peter died and today is his memorial service. Jeff, Peter's boss, told me on the phone last week that people in the office were distracted and upset; they needed closure. And Peter's family began asking about a funeral, because they, too, needed some kind of closure. Ironically, the last thing Anna, Evan, and I want is to memorialize Peter, when we're still trying to understand what happened. But outside of a small group of friends and family, most of those gathering here today think Peter died from a heart attack or something like it. Perhaps if they knew the truth, they would understand why closure, for us at least, is going to take much more time than the length of this memorial service.

So here we are, at the Powerhouse, a community center in the same beach town in which Peter lived. It was, actually, once a power plant, built in the 1920s to supply hot water to a hotel that's long gone. The only thing left from those days is the smokestack that rises into the sky, overlooking the beach. The Powerhouse has a large all-purpose room, open and airy, with polished wood floors that can fit about 120 white folding chairs, which several of my friends came early to help set up and configure into rows.

It's a Thursday afternoon, so most of Peter's colleagues will be here; the firm is providing a shuttle from its office a few miles away. It's been eight work days since he died, and I'm told the firm has reassigned his clients to colleagues and reassigned his secretary; his office was cleaned out and its contents delivered to his house two days ago. I offered to clean it out myself, thinking no one would willingly volunteer for such a gruesome task. I knew what he was likely doing in his office, so I thought it best if I were the one to deal with it. But it had already been done. The speed and efficiency with which the firm has packaged up and erased Peter's existence feels breathtaking to me.

Peter's parents, aunt, sister, and brother are here. Yesterday afternoon I visited his parents at their hotel and steeled myself for an avalanche of tears, for this loss to have broken them open in a million ways. But his parents weren't crying. They were sad, of course, terribly sad, but subdued and composed. Peter's mom and I hugged, and there was mention of God's will and of "being with the Lord now." Ah, yes, I thought. This is what death is like when you have faith, and when that faith is the lens through which you view the world, including life and death. Peter's parents, who were told he died of a heart infection but not how he contracted it, see his death as much as a beginning as an end, the start of his eternal life. I am certain they believe they will see their son again in Heaven. Yet it's this word-for-word belief in the Bible that created a distance between Peter and his parents, and it was something he complained about often over the years.

Anna and Evan are sitting in the front row, holding sheets of paper on which they have composed brief remembrances of their

father. We rehearsed what each of us had written before one another last night. They are holding their speeches in their hands,
their faces expressionless. I know they are exhausted and not
ready to do this. Neither am I.

The twelve days leading up to this service today have been a
living hell of activity: interviewing financial advisers (something I
didn't even know one could do), finding an accountant capable of
filing a host of tax returns that include three years for which Peter
didn't even bother filing, as well as what will be an estate tax return, and then returns for trusts that have yet to be set up. I've
been filling out mountains of forms—financial, insurance, motor
vehicle, Health and Human Services, IRS, COBRA, and on and
on. It's an overwhelming amount of information to process and a
tidal wave of to-do lists. Last week Anna and Evan met for the first
time with the estate's attorney, Jenny Bratt, whom I have hired to
handle the probate work. When the kids and I got to her office,
Jenny and the paralegal that works with her had a handout prepared for each of us, separating probate into its various phases,
trying to break down what is happening and what will happen as
we move forward. It is a long and exhaustive list of items and although I don't know it yet, I won't even be able to get started for
another three months, which is how long it is going to take for
the court to appoint me executor of Peter's estate. And the process of probate—of truly settling that estate—will take nearly two
years.

I have made a list of Peter's assets for Jenny, a list of contrac-
tors who could assess necessary repairs to his house and prepare
bids, met with three realtors, two bank officers, waited in a line
for a death certificate, and found trauma counseling for my kids.
And that's not even the worst of it. The worst of it was Peter's
phone.

It was on his bed when he died, a new, very large iPhone 6

Plus of which I was terrified. It sat in the top drawer of the desk in my office, and each morning at six A.M. the phone's alarm went off, its volume steadily increasing, so that even through two closed doors—my office and my bedroom—I could hear it. I couldn't sleep if it was anywhere near me, so instead I raced from my bed every morning into my office, trying not to wake my kids, pulled the desk drawer open, and grabbed the phone, its screen flashing urgently: "Take Meds!" "Take Meds!" over and over until I turned it off. I couldn't figure out how to disable that alarm.

And then there were the texts from drug dealers, which continued for several days after Peter's death. "Hey bro, need some sprinkles?" and "Where are you?" and "Hey bro, you dead?" I considered texting back: "Bro, I'm dead," but didn't. I could see texts going back months, to and from his dealers, a lapse in judgment it's hard to imagine Peter making. This phone didn't belong to him; it belonged to his law firm. I will obsess over its texts for months, having photographed them, in an effort to identify the dealers, the drugs, the timing of his death.

Peter, May 28, 9:35 A.M: "Can we also get seven of blondie?" to someone whose name was Mike. Between June 8 and June 10, Peter was trying desperately to get something "blonde." (According to a DEA report, "blonde" is slang for cocaine.) Mike asked on June 8: "What are you looking for blonde wise? That way I can do everything at once." Peter asked him to just call. At 6:23 P.M. Mike texted: "Going to be bummed but he said tomorrow for sure. So would you like to do everything tomorrow including the blonde?" Peter responded that he'd been waiting a week already. Mike texted back: "Yes this guy is totally reliable but I guess is just taking a few days extra because you know it's not the easiest thing to come by always. But I know it's totally a bummer when it gets pushed back extra days and stuff and I apologize."

The next day, a Wednesday, a night Anna and Evan stayed at

his house, Peter texted Mike: "Dude . . . Whatup . . . save me here" and finally, at 9:10 that night, Mike responded: "Should be in tonight. You up and ready?" and Peter replied: "Yep yep yep! What's the story? Def waiting and ready tonight." Mike texted back: "I'm ready come over." Peter responded: "Leave here in 5. So see u in 20." I'm wondering what he told the kids that night, or if he just left and didn't say anything.

July 1, 5:55 P.M., a text from Peter to Mike: "Hey bro . . . howz blondie—ready for our date? Even a small one tonight?" He tried again on July 2 at 5:42 P.M.: "You alive there? Where is my girl blondie? Looking for my date ASAP! Lol . . ." And then: "Hey bro, wz sending to ur other text. Looking for a date with Blondie:-) haven't seen Blondie in days!" Some of Peter's texts mention "paper" which I determined means cash. June 4, for instance, Peter wrote: "What is the total amount of paper needed?" the response, this time from a phone number with the area code 808, was: "2550," and then, "Oops I forgot 360 from the pinks. 2900. Sorry." The two of them met somewhere about 2 P.M. that day, a Thursday. When I looked through Peter's bank statements, I saw that he was spending more money on drugs each month, at least for the last several months, than he was paying in support for the kids and me—as much as $8,000 a month.

The texts on Peter's phone were disturbing enough on their own, but there were photos too. One is Peter, shirtless, high as a kite, wild-eyed and silly in a bathroom mirror selfie, and photos of other people, someone standing in front of a toilet, flipping through a magazine, a tourniquet around her arm, just above the elbow. There are photos of Snowball investigating a fully loaded syringe near the edge of the bathroom sink, her little pink ears dropped back and her tail curved up like a comma. The syringe has a torn piece of paper from a yellow-lined legal pad taped around it with the partially visible words "NOT F. . . ." written in capital letters and red marker. There are photos of white-lined notebook paper with a table drawn in Peter's hand, containing the day, time, and dose of injections and a running total, measured in what I assume are milligrams.

NOW HERE WE ARE, with poignant speeches, funny stories, even music. Anna has prepared an emotionally wrenching a capella version of "Blackbird," the only Beatles song Peter ever liked. Last night, when the kids and I were rehearsing our speeches, Anna said she wished we didn't have to do this right now.

"I know," I said. "I wish we didn't have to either. But the people Dad worked with, and Grandma and Grandpa and the rest of the family, want this service too. This isn't for us. This is for everyone else. Like putting on a play." And it is, absurdly, like theatre. What I would really like to say to the audience is "I can clear this up for all of you in five minutes, so you can stop asking for details about what happened and why." But I don't—we don't—because we are afraid to tell anyone the truth. It feels to me that Peter's firm is tiptoeing around the circumstances of his death, and that makes me fear telling the truth to anyone beyond a very small circle of friends and family. I know Wilson Sonsini sent a firm-wide email notifying its employees about Peter's death, posted a note about it on the firm's website, and took down Peter's attorney profile. But I have no idea who there, other than Jeff, knows how he really died.

It could be no one he worked with suspected anything was seriously wrong with Peter, although the needle caps, tourniquet, and alcohol wipes in his work bag suggest he was shooting up in the office. Today, however, is not about conjecture. It's about memorializing. And I will do what I've been asked to do: provide closure. I have orchestrated today's careful performance in which

Peter will be canonized. And then everyone at his firm can get back to billing hours.

Matt, an associate who worked for Peter, comes up to the front of the room and takes the microphone. He has been so shaken by his boss's sudden death he can barely speak, and tears run down his cheeks as he talks about Peter as a mentor and friend. I look around the room to see how his co-workers are taking this heart-breaking display and am stunned. The room is packed and there is a winding staircase that leads to an upper floor where people who did not get seats are standing. Many of them are staring at their phones. They are reading texts and emails, perhaps even reviewing documents on those tiny screens; some of them are actually thumb-typing. Quite a few of those sitting in the back have their heads bent toward their laps, hands clearly cradling phones. Their colleague and friend is dead—for all they know from working too hard—and they can't stop working long enough to listen to what is being said about him.

It's possible that this is how they are coping with the unex-pected death of their fifty-one-year-old colleague. Research from Larry Richard, an organizational psychologist, former attorney and founder of LawyerBrain, a consultancy that uses data about the personalities of lawyers to enhance their performance, shows that in general, lawyers are hooked on intellectual validation—that little shot of dopamine they get every time they solve a cli-ent's problem. Dopamine makes us feel better; being needed by someone, even a client, makes us feel important. Maybe the at-torneys here believe being needed will act as a hedge against their own mortality. How can you die if your clients are emailing you requests for opinion letters and document reviews? How can you die if you have a conference call on your calendar that afternoon? But, of course, you can.

When I took Peter's phone off of his bed, I looked at the call history to see the last person with whom he spoke. When you're dying, I wondered, who do you call? Peter dialed in to a conference call.

I phoned the number to identify it and found it was a conference line, the kind of number you dial and then are prompted to enter a pin number, after which you are connected to others in the conference. The last call of Peter's life wasn't to his kids, me, his parents, a friend, even one of his dealers. Peter—drifting in and out of consciousness and barely able to sit up—had dialed in to a work call.

He very nearly predicted this would happen. Right before Peter became a partner at Wilson, when we were still married, he told me he couldn't see himself working this intensely long-term. "I can't do this for the next twenty years," he said. "I can't physically do it."

Dysfunctional corporate culture isn't unique to law firms. Jeffrey Pfeffer, a professor at Stanford Business School and author of the book *Dying for a Paycheck,* said when he held a position on the Committee for Faculty and Staff Human Resources, he was struck by the fact that Stanford's wellness program focused on exercise and eating better when all of the behaviors that caused people to be unhealthy—overdrinking, overeating, drugs—were caused by their work environment. "The corporate workplace has become increasingly inhumane," he said. "No one gives a shit about people. Forty, fifty, sixty years ago, organizations used to be communities. They're not anymore. That ended in the eighties, with the takeover movement, the financialization of everything. We live in a much more transactional world."

The memorial service finishes and people say their goodbyes. A group of lawyers that worked with Peter over the years head to a bar across the street to reminisce about and glorify a man they didn't really know. Peter's siblings head to their deceased brother's house to spend the night. Evan is staying there, too, so he can drive his uncle to the airport in the morning.

About midnight my phone rings. It's Evan, and I can tell from his voice he is frightened. Unable to sleep, he went downstairs to poke through some of Peter's things in the mudroom. He is trying to figure out who his dad was.

Evan saw an earthenware vase Peter has had forever and in which he stored old pens, business cards, paper clips, and other odds and ends. It was sitting in a shoebox with some other junk, tucked behind boots, shoes, badminton rackets, and a deflated football. Evan emptied it onto the floor to look more closely at what was inside. He saw a thin piece of gold foil that appeared to have been ripped from the liner of a cigarette box, folded carefully, about the size of a pat of butter. He unfolded it. Inside were what looked like quartz pebbles. "Mom," Evan says in a whisper, "I'm pretty sure it's crystal meth. I took a photo of it and searched online and that is what came up. It looks just like the pictures. I'm kind of scared. What should I do? What if it's on my hands now? Can something happen to you if it gets on your skin?"

Crystal meth is the common name for crystal methamphetamine, which is usually smoked in a small glass pipe, but it can also be snorted, swallowed, or injected.

I tell Evan not to worry. "I think you just don't want it near your mouth or nose," I say, although I have no idea if that's true, because at that moment I still don't know anything about the drug. I don't know if you smoke, snort, or shoot meth—maybe you do all three. Maybe you can eat it too. "Just wrap it back up and put it in the vase and wash your hands really well. I'll be up there tomorrow and I'll take it and get rid of it," I tell him.

"I wish I hadn't stayed here tonight," he says, his voice weak. "It's really creepy. I just don't want to be here." I ask if he wants to come home right now. I tell him he can come back tonight, and I will get his uncle a cab to the airport tomorrow morning or go up there myself and drive him. But Evan feels he should stay until the morning and say a proper goodbye.

I hang up the phone but there is no sleep for me. I hadn't known Peter was using methamphetamine too. I Google it and stare at endless photos of methamphetamine addicts, recognizing in those agonized faces some of what I saw in Peter—the jaundiced look of his eyes, the yellow-brown stains on his teeth, his accelerating hair loss, the sores on his hands and the side of his face.

Long after the memorial service I speak to David Epstein— a scientist at the National Institute on Drug Abuse who heads its assessment, prediction, and treatment unit—about Peter's descent into addiction, confounding because outwardly at least, he had a good life and still it did not bring him what he needed.

"You mentioned that Peter told you he couldn't see himself going on like this for the next twenty years," Epstein says over the phone from his office in Washington, D.C. "I think addiction is primarily something that happens to people that look at the landscape of alternatives available to them in the present and the future, what will be available to them in any foreseeable amount of time, and if none of it looks good," he says. "They run out of reasons not to try drugs."

PART III

 TWELVE

Big Law's Big Problems

PETER GRADUATED AT THE top of his class from law school in May 1997 and couldn't wait to leave it behind him. Although he had always been somewhat melancholy, after law school he seemed consistently down, and those lows became more intense and darker as time went on.

A landmark study of substance use and the mental health concerns of lawyers conducted in 2016 by the Hazelden Betty Ford Foundation and the American Bar Association found that nearly 30 percent of lawyers suffer from depression, almost 20 percent from anxiety. The question on the survey asked about symptoms in the last twelve months, but when lawyers are asked about depression over the course of their careers, the figure is usually more than 40 percent, says Daniel Lukasik, who founded the website Lawyers with Depression in 2007, after he was diagnosed with major depression.

Lukasik, who was a practicing attorney for twenty-five years, struggled with the disorder for much of his life but wasn't diagnosed until he was forty. Now he is director of workplace well-being for Mental Health Advocates of Western New York and also runs discussion groups for attorneys struggling with depression and anxiety. "A common thread in the groups I run is the gap between what people thought the law was going to be and what it has become for them," says Lukasik.

The most common personality type for lawyers is "INTJ," according to research conducted by LawyerBrain's Larry Richard. It stands for introverted, intuitive, thinking, judging and is also one of the least common personality types among the general public. Richard has more than 25,000 sets of data on the personalities of lawyers and describes the typical mind-set as a "negativity mindset," which is essential, he says, for practicing law. "Lawyers are always looking for problems and do that by thinking dispassionately and being alert to irregularity—what is wrong, what could go wrong—and by being suspicious about people's motives and agendas," says Richard. The profession attracts people who are more negative, more skeptical, and more pessimistic than the average person.

Depression, along with anxiety and intense stress, likely has something to do with the high rate of suicide in the legal profession, the fourth highest compared to other professions, according to a 2014 analysis by CNN (using data from the Centers for Disease Control and Prevention, also known as the CDC). Studies have shown that years of unrelenting work stress can damage the prefrontal cortex, which we use for problem-solving, emotional control, verbal communication, and to form memories. Anna Rose Childress, director of the Brain-Behavioral Vulnerabilities Division of the Center for Studies on Addiction at the University of Pennsylvania, says chronic stress can make us more vulnerable to depression. "Stress reduces the ability to manage the dark side of life, the slings and arrows, the difficulties we face," Childress says. "And that shows up in the form of depression or anxiety."

In October 2018, forty-two-year-old attorney Gabriel MacConaill was crumbling under a mountain of stress. MacConaill, a bankruptcy partner at the firm Sidley Austin in Los Angeles, was in the midst of a big bankruptcy case. The previous year, MacConaill's mentor and two other attorneys in the bankruptcy practice group had left the firm, and his wife, Joanna Litt, says he felt overwhelmed with work. In the weeks leading up to the bankruptcy filing, she recalls, it was largely her husband and one other partner doing all the work. On October 14, a Sunday afternoon, MacConaill told his wife he had to run to the office for a few hours. He kissed Litt goodbye, drove his car into the office parking lot, and shot himself in the head. November would have been the couple's ten-year wedding anniversary. A month later Litt wrote about her husband's suicide in *The American Lawyer*. Her open letter to the magazine was titled "Big Law Killed My Husband."

MacConaill and Litt met on the first day of law school and he, like Peter, graduated at the top of his class. Litt wrote that her husband was "the smartest person I ever met. He was also the kindest, most selfless person I've ever met." MacConaill struggled with a drinking problem—intermittent binge drinking—something Litt now suspects was masking a deeper pain. He also had severe anxiety, was a perfectionist, and—although Litt didn't understand it at the time—was likely battling depression.

One night about two weeks before his suicide, MacConaill had been at the office more than twelve hours. Late that evening, on the phone with his wife, he said he felt as if his body was "failing" him. Litt got in her car and went to pick him up and take him to the emergency room. "Gabe got in the car and said, 'If we go to the ER, that's the end of my career,'" Litt told me. "But I knew he wasn't thinking right, he was dehydrated and exhausted." Litt even hired a nurse to administer fluids to MacConaill intravenously when he was home—which wasn't often during this period—and his doctor prescribed Ambien to help MacConaill sleep. But Litt says the damage was done.

"That case was what finally did it," she tells me, crying and so engulfed by grief and pain I can feel it through the phone. "Big Law has a very toxic culture. In fact, we had talked about him just getting through this case and then figuring out what he wanted to do from there, how to get out. We talked about it extensively." In her *American Lawyer* essay she wrote about urging MacConaill to quit, writing that he hadn't smiled in weeks, wasn't sleeping, and everything he said was negative. But he told Litt he couldn't quit in the middle of a case. She noted the irony that he found it easier to kill himself than quit his job.

"Here's the thing," Litt says. "You've got these individuals who really feel like if they make that kind of move, if they leave Big Law, they are a failure. And I think Gabe looked at it as if he'd be failing too."

LAW SCHOOLS DEVELOP LAWYERS, yes, but they also develop leaders; lawyers in this country play a very visible and influential role in private and public life. According to the American Bar Association, twenty-six U.S. presidents were also lawyers, and that includes Thomas Jefferson, John Adams, Abraham Lincoln, Theodore Roosevelt, Bill Clinton, and Barack Obama. The legal profession has not only supplied the majority of American presidents but also, in recent decades, almost half of Congress.

Lawyers occupy leadership roles as governors, state legislators, judges, prosecutors, general counsels of corporations, managing partners of law firms, and CEOs. For better or worse, they maintain our justice system and, in many ways, are responsible for preserving the most important aspects of our societal fabric.

Yet law students get little leadership training. Deborah L. Rhode, a professor at Stanford Law School and director of its Center on the Legal Profession, says the majority of lawyers lack the "soft skills" needed to be effective leaders, like self-awareness and emotional intelligence. Instead, law schools wind up changing many students' worldview and goals. The goals they had when they entered law school become less centered around justice and more focused on winning.

Elizabeth Mertz, an anthropologist and law professor at the University of Wisconsin Law School who has studied the pedagogy of law school, writes that first-year law students experience an often "jarring confrontation with the worldview and practices of a new profession."

In 2007, Mertz analyzed the language in a full semester of contracts classes at eight law schools. In her book *The Language of Law School: Learning to "Think Like a Lawyer"* she examines the way legal language changes how a law student (and eventually, a lawyer) actually understands a story—a client's story, their opposing counsel's story, even their own personal story. And the change, Mertz writes, is profound. "There are entirely new views of reality and authority, new landmarks and ways of speaking, altered conceptions of themselves and others (and their relations to the world around them) packed quietly into the reading lessons students encounter in the first-year law school curriculum."

One of Peter's good friends during law school was a guy named Chris, who graduated number two in their class. During his first year of law school Chris, like Peter, felt as if he had been hit by a truck. Aside from the intense pressure and exhaustion from keeping up with the reading, Chris says law school taught him and Peter to turn their minds into "finely honed intellectual weapons. Everything suddenly became a competition and we were constantly comparing and contrasting," he says. "How do you pull yourself out of that mind-set? It invades every aspect of your being, and ends up hurting you and those closest to you."

Nine years after law school graduation Chris was arrested for obstructing a drug investigation, after hiding an "eight-ball" (3.5 grams) of cocaine for his dealer, who was also one of his clients. At the time of his arrest Chris was working as a private criminal defense attorney in a mid-Atlantic state, having served first as an assistant public defender and assistant state's attorney. He was also deep into addiction, snorting three eight-balls of cocaine and swallowing between fifty and seventy pills, usually Percocet or the opioid Tylox, each month. I tracked him down in New England, where he is slowly rebuilding his law practice. After his conviction and disbarment in 2006, Chris was sentenced to two years of probation (one of which he spent in home detention). He was recently readmitted to the bar. "You know, if I hadn't been arrested I would have been smoking rocks and shooting up too, just like Peter," he tells me as I'm leaving his office. "I would honestly have put a needle in my arm, I know it. I was buying coke, I was buying so much coke, and I remember thinking: I shouldn't be doing this. But it was all about feeling better."

Peter certainly wanted to feel better. He was miserable both as a law student and a lawyer (he refused to even drive through New Hampshire ever again), and lived for each small success—a pat on the back from a professor, a client, an email acknowledging a job well done from a partner. It was the start of his addiction to whatever made him feel better, some small shot of dopamine that helped ease the constant self-doubt that plagued him.

———

BEFORE THEY ENTER LAW school, prospective law students are actually healthier than the general population, both physically and mentally. "There is good data showing that they drink less than other young people, use less substances, have much less depression, and are much less hostile," says Andy Benjamin, an affiliate professor of law and a clinical psychology professor at the University of Washington in Seattle. Benjamin has led several research teams over the past thirty years in studying law student health and well-being. "Law students are a bellwether for the profession, that's what our data show," he says. They are the canary in the legal coal mine; if law students aren't doing well, the profession isn't doing well either.

In the 2014 Survey of Law Student Well-Being, researchers surveyed 11,000 law students at fifteen American law schools and found a high incidence of drinking (41 percent had engaged in binge drinking in the previous two weeks), drug use, depression, anxiety, and suicide risk. Overall, 14 percent of students had used a prescription drug without a prescription in the previous year, most frequently stimulants (the most common was Adderall). Almost 40 percent of students tested positive for anxiety—14 percent for severe anxiety.

In 2018, the American Bar Association named March 28 National Mental Health Day at law schools nationwide, in an effort to lessen the stigma of depression and anxiety in the profession. A month later, in April, Harvard Law School released the results of its first annual survey of student mental health. Among the 886 respondents, 25 percent suffered from depression (in the general population 7.7 percent of those ages 20–39 suffer from depression) and 20 percent were at heightened risk of suicide.

Two of the best-known researchers to study how law school affects law students are Lawrence S. Krieger, a professor of law at Florida State University College of Law, and Kennon M. Sheldon, a professor of psychological sciences at the University of Missouri. In February 2015—just five months before Peter died—the pair published a paper titled "What Makes Lawyers Happy?" in the *George Washington Law Review*. Their research discovered that right after students begin law school they experience a significant spike in depression and negativity, as well as corresponding decreases in positive affect and life satisfaction. Students' values and their motivation for becoming lawyers shift in the first year of law school, from internal values such as helping others and being community-oriented to more superficial and external values and motivation, like money, recognition, or pleasing and impressing others. And those values stick with them.

After Peter and I left New Hampshire and law school life, I assumed the days of all-nighters and nonstop exhaustion were over. During the previous three years, I blamed our lack of a family life on the overwhelming demands and pressures of law school. With that behind us, I assumed Peter and I would do things like have dinner together after putting the baby to bed, maybe find a sitter and go to a movie now and then, take weekend walks on the beach, our daughter nestled into the little backpack we had bought for her. That was not to be. One night, about two months into his new job, Peter didn't come home from the office. I woke up early in the morning and saw that his side of the bed was undisturbed, so I called his cell phone—a Motorola flip phone back then—and he picked up right away. "Where are you?" I asked. "You never came home last night. You never called. What happened? Are you okay?" Peter said he was fine, he had slept in his office, on the floor under his desk. He had to deliver the draft of something—a brief or a memo—that morning and decided to just stay all night and work on it. Anna was eleven months old; we had been in San Diego four months.

When he got home that night, I asked him why, as a lawyer

now, he still had to pull an all-nighter. I assumed those happened only in law school, a rite of passage. Peter, exhausted, said no, they happened whenever something needed to get done and there was no other way to get it done. "You're kidding," I said. "You're going to have to spend all night sometimes in your office, the same as you did in the law school library? I can't believe that. I thought that was over."

Peter was exasperated. "Over?" he said. "No, Eilene, it's never *over*." I knew that after working nearly thirty-two hours straight he was mentally and physically fried. But I didn't understand why an attorney, an adult man, would sleep overnight on his office floor. Didn't Peter have any control over his schedule? Didn't they know he had a daughter? A wife? A home?

Peter looked at me. "I'm a first-year associate, Eilene. This is what I have to do. What did you think it was going to be like?" he asked.

"Not like this," I said.

"Well, get used to it," he snapped, "because this is the way it is."

TO COPE WITH THE long hours and intense stress—as well as the resulting depression and anxiety—many lawyers turn to alcohol and, increasingly, to drugs. In April 2018, I posted a query on TopLawSchools.com, a popular collection of forums for law students and attorneys, asking if they would discuss, anonymously and candidly, their experience with drug use and/or abuse in the legal profession. (Despite its name, TLS receives thousands of posts from practicing lawyers.) I chose this route because it had proven impossible to get a lawyer to go on record talking about drug use.

The 2016 ABA/Hazelden Betty Ford study of alcohol and drug use in the legal profession surveyed nearly 13,000 practicing attorneys in 19 states but only 3,400 answered the questions about drug use. I wondered why 75 percent of attorneys skipped over that section. Patrick Krill, the study's lead author, told me it certainly wasn't because 75 percent of lawyers don't use drugs. "I believe they were afraid to answer," he said. Since people posting comments on the TLS site do not reveal their names nor the firms for which they work—instead identifying as "anonymous user" or creating a handle for themselves—their comments are often brutally honest.

Lawyers responding to my TLS query wrote that opioids and coke are often used to make hangovers bearable, that they and many of their colleagues use Adderall for focus (not prescribed for them). There is a lot of marijuana use and drinking. Underlying it all, one commenter wrote, is the addiction to work. "Everything else is just derivative of that. Of course, some people have underlying substance abuse problems. In the end though, firm life is the addiction. You are a total slave to the work."

Kevin Chandler, director of the Hazelden Betty Ford Foundation's Legal Professionals Program in Center City, Minnesota, tells me about a client he spoke with recently, a female partner in a large law firm who also has three small children. "She was very put-together, very professional. And she said, 'I broke into three of my neighbors' houses looking for opioid pills.' Many of these lawyers start with prescription drugs, and at first take them as prescribed. But I think the profession is so stressful that they start using them for relief—opioids, Ambien, cocaine, Adderall, Xanax. We see it all."

There were certainly things about legal work that Peter liked, mostly the intellectual challenge it provided. There were always interesting problems to solve and he was good at it. But he felt that the example set for him by the partners he admired, and in whose steps he longed to follow, was that life outside of work—

like family and personal time, social and emotional connections, spirituality—would have to be put aside. So that's what Peter did too. And over the years he became more negative and combative than I had ever seen him. Research from psychologist Martin E. P. Seligman, founder of the field of positive psychology and director of the Positive Psychology Center at the University of Pennsylvania, shows that emotions like anger, jealousy, and anxiety serve a role for lawyers—they narrow the social and cognitive environment, which helps them maintain an unwavering drive to win.

"The legal field encourages antagonism in ways other fields don't," wrote one lawyer on TopLawSchools.com. "Lawyers are expected to be argumentative about everything, so it's not seen as weird if a guy is willing to rip someone to shreds over a typo. And it's expected that lawyers will rip each other to shreds to show a company that their firm is the best one to get the job done. So all the games and undermining/one-upping is seen as part of the sport."

A big contributor to Peter's growing negativity was his wait to become a partner. After nine years as an associate working sixty to eighty hours a week, he was counting on being elected a member (his firm calls its equity partners members), but in November 2006 was told that wouldn't happen until the following year. Peter was furious and resentful about the decision to delay his promotion. He felt he had given the profession everything he had for nearly a decade, and now he was being asked to wait another year to become a partner. This kind of thing was—and is— happening in many other firms too, both because of post-recession economic realities and because, in most large law firms, wealth is concentrated at the top, among the most senior partners.

Although Peter was given a vague reason for his delayed promotion—someone was up for promotion ahead of him, and that would fill the San Diego office's quota for new members that year—sometimes the reason is very clear. Sarah, an attorney who had spent seven years working her way toward an equity partnership at a prestigious Am Law 100 firm (the top 100 law firms in the U.S., as ranked by *American Lawyer* magazine) in Southern California, knew why she had been passed over. About five years earlier she became pregnant with her son, and after she shared this news with her colleagues, a female partner took her aside to speak to her privately. This partner told Sarah a story about a friend's abortion, saying it was "no big deal" and then asking if Sarah's husband would be upset if Sarah did the same thing.

"I was shocked," Sarah tells me. "I said, 'Well, this pregnancy was planned, we are in our thirties, married, own a home and have jobs, so yes, I think my husband would find it strange if I had an abortion.' And this partner said, 'Well, that's disappointing—my husband believes in a woman's right to choose.' I answered that we were pro-choice too, and our choice was to keep the baby." Sarah had a son and two years later, a daughter, at a point in her career when she could have been promoted but wasn't. Sarah says the partner who had suggested an abortion "told me multiple times that I would not be accepted into the partnership because I took 'too many leaves.' I took two maternity leaves." Her story illustrates the intense competition among associates aspiring to a shrinking number of equity partnerships at big firms.

Between 2008 and 2012, the legal profession experienced layoffs, salary decreases, and hiring freezes. Firms still hire new attorneys, but the number being promoted to equity partner is shrinking, thanks to the creation of a new class of partner, the "non-equity" or "income" partner. (Since equity is an ownership interest in a business, partners without equity aren't really partners because they don't own a piece of the firm.)

Every night in 2006, Peter came home from work livid, would eat his dinner and complain about his clients, his colleagues, and the firm's management. How much of his unhappiness was due to ten years in the profession, the delayed partnership, or other factors like genetics or his specific brain chemistry is impossible to know. Long before becoming an attorney he described himself as a "glass-half-empty kind of guy." I remember the day our daughter, Anna, was born and the obstetrician handed her warm little body to me. Peter, watching, wiping tears from his eyes, said, "Well, we'll be lucky if she's not pregnant and a drug addict at fifteen." Both the obstetrician and I gasped.

Peter looked at the doctor and me, embarrassed. "No, no, I don't want any of those things for her, of course not," he explained. "I'm just being realistic." But that wasn't realistic, it was *pessimistic*. In almost every undertaking pessimism is considered maladaptive, but not in the law, writes psychologist Martin Seligman. There is little upside to this, aside from winning cases. Lawyers' pessimism and disenchantment leaves them in poor health, wrote Seligman. "They are at much greater risk than the general population for depression, heart disease, alcoholism, and illegal drug use."

■ THIRTEEN

White-Collar Pill Popping

THE HANDFUL OF PEOPLE who knew the truth about Peter's drug abuse and death in 2015 were stunned because of the height from which he fell, and that his power and wealth did not protect him. They figured it was a one-off, that in the mortality statistics that have come to define the addiction epidemic in this country, Peter's death was an outlier.

But it wasn't. It is part of a much bigger societal problem and it certainly wasn't a one-off for me. It remains the most significant and tragic event of my life, upending everything, including my identity and my orientation to the world.

After probate concluded in November 2016 and my son was off to college, I sold my house and moved back to the place I was born—New York City—to get some distance from San Diego and all it represented. I wanted to begin my life again. So much of it up until that point had been determined by Peter's choices about his career, how and where he wanted to live and, in many ways, who he wanted to be. I went along with those choices not because I believed they were right for me but because I was afraid of the alternative, of *any* alternative. The big decisions in my life up until Peter's death were made from a place of fear, and that place was deep within my own psyche. I was afraid of people I loved leaving me or not loving me back, of them not liking me, afraid of not being able to manage on my own, afraid to make decisions I believed would almost certainly be bad ones, of raising kids the wrong way, of sounding stupid when I spoke, of not having the earning power to support myself. I didn't have much faith in my ability to make my own choices; I usually assumed they would be wrong.

Peter's death forced me to take a long, hard look at my life. I had spent the last twenty-five years seeking his approval and validation. I needed him to tell me or show me I *mattered*, that I was smart, a good mother, writer, wife, human being—you name it, I needed him to make it feel true. But how could he? How could Peter acknowledge how hard I worked when he was so incredibly overworked himself, and thought that no one felt more isolated and stressed than he did? In his mind, I think, to even recognize that I also worked hard, that I, too, was exhausted and stressed and lonely, would have taken some of his power away.

After we divorced, Peter was still the barometer by which I judged my own forward movement. My goal changed from getting him to acknowledge my importance in our life to proving that I didn't need him. I wanted, so badly, to make him see that I could find love and success and happiness on my own and in my own way. Once he died I couldn't operate that way anymore. I felt completely unmoored.

What was the point, then, of everything? What were my goals now? Where would I get my motivation? It had been anger pushing me forward, anger that enabled me to do things I hadn't believed I could—and that Peter hadn't believed I would—like finalize a divorce, date again, create a financial plan for my future, refinance my mortgage, expand my freelance business. The year Peter died, I finally reached my annual income goal of $70,000—the minimum amount I calculated I would need to live in San Diego without alimony and child support. And it was anger, once again, that helped me put aside my grief and plow ahead with all the tasks involved in settling Peter's estate and cleaning up the messes he left behind.

A couple of years before Peter's death, I started meditating regularly at a Zen Buddhist center. I had become more self-reflective, both to cope with all the changes in my life after divorce and as a way to understand what went wrong in my marriage and move beyond that to something better. My efforts got derailed, however, by the chaos of Peter's life and its effect on mine and those of our children. But after his death, in the two years I spent tying up the loose ends of his life, I also grabbed hold of my own loose ends and tried to figure out how to tie those up, too.

I did a lot of EMDR therapy—watching that little spot of light travel back and forth across a screen—and I wrote. I wrote down everything I was seeing and feeling, and tried to make sense of it on the page, which is the way I tend to process the world around me. I cried a lot. I spent time hiking alone, walking the beach near what used to be Peter's house, thinking. I leaned heavily on my friends for support and understanding. Elisabeth Kübler-Ross famously defined five stages of grief, but mine hasn't followed such an organized trajectory. Instead I feel many things—anger, relief, sadness, disbelief, fear, anxiety—mixed together in different combinations at different times. I can be relieved at the peacefulness in my life without Peter and at the same time miss him, especially when one of our children reaches a new milestone—our son's high school graduation, our daughter's twenty-first birthday.

Yet as the anger I felt after Peter's death abates, I feel, as strange as it might sound, as if there is more space inside me. Without him physically in my life anymore, I'm not always playing defense. I no longer have to brace myself for whatever intellectual condescension or financial bullying or irrational behavior he is going to sling my way. Instead, my head fills with memories and reflection and a deep sadness. Every time I'm out hiking in the woods, marveling at how beautiful it is, I also think of Peter, of how much he would like it. I had never gone camping until I met him, never hiked a mountain trail. I spent ten years trying to learn to ski because Peter enjoyed it so much. He used to ski halfway down a mountain and stop, go a bit off trail and light a cigarette, enjoying a smoke while taking in the view. He loved the wilderness, especially the woods of upstate New York.

I was driving in that direction recently, on a cold, rainy autumn day. The air was heavy and misty, the trees hanging on to their last few leaves. I stopped at a gas station and saw, across the barely paved road, a couple of double-wide trailer homes. I got out of the car to pump gas and smelled cigarette smoke; a classic rock station was playing Guns N' Roses. After I paid, I sat in the driver's seat crying. God I miss him, I thought. I miss that time. I miss the smells and sounds. But I think what I miss most is something Peter and I had so little of—a loving, mutually supportive, I've-got-your-back-and-you've-got-mine kind of relationship. The opportunity for that existed back then, in our early years together, along with our naivete about all the ways things could and would go wrong. Our future had loomed large and thrilling to us, and it would be a long time before we knew anything about the complications of life as a married couple, as parents, as people in midlife, mid-career, midstream.

Perhaps the most profound thing to happen to me since Peter's death, the result of both finding his body and cleaning out his house, was understanding and accepting that death would eventually be my fate too. Not in the same way, but I am, indeed, going to die at some point. For the first time in my life I am coming to terms with my own mortal existence, part and parcel of what it means to be human. It's a fact I suspect most of us rarely acknowledge.

It seems to me that many of us spend more time and energy thinking about things we want or the things we want to buy, than how we want to live and die. I remember the day I held an estate sale at Peter's house and sold almost all his furniture in four hours—about $35,000 worth for $7,500. The furniture and art and special silverware he had carefully chosen so that the interior of the house reflected his tastes as much as the outside wound up in someone's U-Haul. Some of it I couldn't even give away. No one would take the frosted glass and chrome computer table, or the full-length gold-leaf mirror that leaned against his bedroom wall. When I sold Peter's beloved dining table, the one crafted from a thick, contiguous piece of partially split wood, it brought to life the saying "You can't take it with you." Peter had marveled at that giant slab, cracks and dark whorls and all, held together with iron crossbars for stability. After he died, this $7,000 table sold for $450 to someone who could disassemble it and had a truck big enough to accommodate it. The iron base was so heavy, no one else was willing to try to get it down the stairs.

During those months of inventorying, cleaning, and selling, I found myself thinking a lot about the trajectory of my own life. Did I want to continue living the way I had been? Was my work still meaningful to me? I used to look at journalism as a kind of calling, a way to be of service by bringing stories of consequence into the public eye. But if I was honest, my journalism wasn't really doing much of that. I had become a reporter who made a living largely by writing about entrepreneurship, start-ups, and new technology. I came to feel I was just adding to the existing noise in American culture about success, innovation, productivity, and efficiency.

After my marriage ended I became a volunteer at the Monarch School, a K–12 school for homeless children near the Mexican border, and it made me feel more committed than ever to trying to help others, especially the disenfranchised. I had already begun, years before Peter's death, to write more stories about social and political issues, like profiles of Marines seriously injured in the Iraq War and new treatments for their post-traumatic stress disorder, sexual assault on college campuses and the subsequent rise of campus feminism. It was the kind of writing I had always been drawn to and found truly gratifying.

Just as I was starting to understand all this about myself, I was also working hard to process the experience of Peter's death. And that meant coming to terms with how acutely disturbing it was to me that he died alone. This fact came up all the time in EMDR therapy and it haunted my dreams—literally. While sleeping, I would see Peter at the end of his life, in pain, sick to his stomach, vomiting. In my dreams he is doubled over, unable to see clearly, stumbling about trying to find a place to lie down. I'm a bystander, watching but not able to reach him. All around me are the things, oddly enough, I don't remember seeing but now know were there—the flattened boxes, the discarded opened mail, the mouse habitat in pieces everywhere. When I'm dreaming, my mind remembers all the things it can't remember when I'm conscious. And then I wake up holding on to the bits and pieces. It is one of the reasons I put so much effort into reconstructing the last hours of Peter's life—trying to prove to myself that he was too high to feel anything, or that he died suddenly, his heart just stopping, with no time to be afraid or think about what was happening or feel regret over what he was losing or had left unsaid.

I knew Peter so intimately and, at one point in my life, loved him so deeply, it is unbearable to think of him alone at the end. Not so much that he might have been in pain, but far more, that he might have been frightened. I think that if I had been there—even if I couldn't have saved him—I could have provided some comfort. I could have held his hand.

In January 2017, I move into an apartment in New York City and begin a part-time graduate program for a master's degree in social work, with an eye toward eventually doing some work in end-of-life care. I don't intend to stop writing; I just want to write about something different, about what it means to be human today, to pursue answers to questions about life, death, addiction, recovery, hate, love, justice, and joy. Before I can do any of that, though, I need to understand Peter's death beyond the personal, in a bigger context. I need to see where his story—the drug-related death of a white-collar, affluent, and outwardly successful professional—fits into the larger story of drug use and abuse in America. It is the only story I can think about and the one I need to write first, before any others.

WHEN I START MY research, I feel sure that Peter's death isn't an outlier at all but the edge of an unidentified trend—white-collar addiction. Then I find an article titled "White-Collar Pill Party" by Bruce Jackson, published in *The Atlantic* magazine in August 1966, almost fifty years before Peter died.

The story shows its age—the way people speak, the copious use of the word *junkie,* the portrayal of women. And while it seems very 1960s, it's also very twenty-first century.

With unknowing prescience, Jackson wrote in 1966: "A lot of

people take a lot more pills than they have any reason to. They think in terms of pills. And so do their physicians: You fix a fat man by giving him a diet pill, you fix a chronic insomniac by giving him a sleeping pill. The publicity goes to the junkies ... but these account for only a small portion of the American drug problem. Far more worrisome are the millions of people who have become dependent on commercial drugs. The junkie *knows* he's hooked; the housewife on amphetamine and the businessman on meprobamate [precursors to benzodiazepines like Xanax and Klonopin] hardly ever realize what has gone wrong."

Two months after Peter died, Theodore J. Cicero, a professor of psychiatry at Washington University School of Medicine and an expert on addiction, published a paper in the journal *Cerebrum* titled "No End in Sight: The Abuse of Prescription Narcotics." He wrote: "Other than the obvious high, what purpose do these drugs serve that accounts for their popularity? It turns out that the initial potent high is not really what most users seek. Rather, narcotics relieve anxiety or depression by providing a short-lived escape from difficult circumstances." Since the 1970s, Cicero has published more than 200 articles on substance abuse; in the last fifteen years he has focused on the epidemiology of opiate abuse. The initial high for an addict is pure bliss, writes Cicero. "But pure bliss becomes an elusive goal and does not repair emotional dysfunction and unpleasant circumstances."

According to the CDC, more than 70,000 Americans died from drug overdoses in 2018. The vast majority of those deaths resulted from synthetic opioids like fentanyl being mixed into black market heroin, cocaine, methamphetamines, and benzodiazepines. By their own admission, more than two million people in the United States have opioid-use disorders, according to a recent government phone survey, and that number is likely an undercount because (among other reasons) not everyone with a drug problem has a telephone. After Peter's death I wanted to learn more about drug use by professionals like him—not only lawyers but investment bankers, doctors, nurses, hedge fund managers, technology company executives, software engineers, and the like—because I find their drug use the most perplexing.

If people in white-collar professional jobs, who are among our society's most well-educated, driven, and high-achieving citizens, are becoming addicts, what does that say about us as a society? I ask myself, what is the point of being here at all, of striving to achieve success in careers and personal lives if so many want to escape once they get there?

I begin interviewing as many professionals as I can to find out which drugs they use and why. I am looking for some common denominator to help explain why they would take the risk and to help me understand why Peter did. Some of the professionals I interview know they have a drug problem but aren't seeking help. Many are in recovery, and others use but feel they don't have a problem. For the latter group, drugs are simply a hack—a short-cut—a way to be more productive, more focused, less depressed, less anxious, more chill, more social, less bored, more creative, just *better*, without having to go through the uncomfortable process of self-examination and self-reflection. Without having to, for example, get more sleep, eat healthier, meditate, spend time with family and friends, get a psychiatric evaluation and treatment. Those things take time, and time is one thing many of those in this group feel is in short supply.

PROFESSIONALS ABUSE DRUGS AND alcohol for many different reasons, but one I heard often was a longing for something more, something different. Something *else*. Right after Peter died, Ben, a highly successful criminal defense attorney in his early fifties,

was arrested for possession of methamphetamine. Two years earlier, Ben was living in an East Coast suburb and had a comfortable life with his wife of three decades, Penny, a doctor. That year,
though, Ben became withdrawn. He was losing weight, dying his
hair, dressing oddly, making humming noises, and had developed a twitch. He started taking unexplained business trips and
often stayed out late into the night, saying he was working. Penny
thought Ben might be having an affair. Then his colleagues began
calling her, saying Ben wasn't showing up for court, and when he
did, he looked like he had slept in a ditch the night before. Some-
time in the middle of 2015, Ben just stopped coming home. By
that point, Penny had cycled through a host of explanations: a
midlife crisis, Huntington's disease, adult-onset Tourette's syn-
drome, frontotemporal dementia, and finally, she believed, her
husband had a brain tumor, because the symptoms seemed to
indicate that. She enlisted the help of her brother to try to coax
Ben into seeing a doctor, but Ben refused to go. On the way home
from that unsuccessful attempt, Penny's brother called and asked,
"Are you sure Ben's not taking meth?" Her brother worked in law
enforcement; he felt his brother-in-law's appearance resembled
that of the meth addicts he arrested.

"I said no," Penny told me. "I had married my own diagnosis.
I was convinced it was a brain tumor. Meth was completely outside of my experience and he wasn't a drug user." It wasn't until
her husband was arrested, in the fall of 2015, that Penny learned
the truth. Ben is now in recovery and drug-free; I ask him why he
started using in the first place.

"I was at a point where I had done everything I wanted to do,
my life was so good," he says. "But there was this middle-age,
crazy feeling I had, thinking, is this all there is? I think of the
opening lines of Dante's *The Divine Comedy*: 'At the mid-point of
the path through life, I found myself lost in a wood so dark, the

way ahead was blotted out [*sic*].' It was like that; I went down a dark rabbit hole." Meth gave Ben "a sense of euphoria and power and clarity" at a moment in his life, he says, when he took everything good in it for granted. "I had worked all these years to establish myself and was at this sort of a pinnacle, and I was like, 'Now what?'"

Ben's reasons for using meth—that "now what?" brand of emptiness or boredom—aren't all that different from the reasons Tony, a slim man in his mid-thirties with a master's degree in quantitative analytics, originally sought out something to make him feel better.

Tony is a vice president at a hedge fund in New York City; he has been taking Adderall, the amphetamine used to treat attention deficit disorders, since 2012, when he was in his late twenties. In the finance industry, cocaine has historically been the stimulant of choice, but as finance jobs become more demanding, the industry's drugs of choice now include "performance enhancers," like Adderall and Vyvanse.

Tony was prescribed Adderall by a psychiatrist with whom he had met to discuss depression. "I had a great life, but I still felt sad," Tony recalls. He chose investment banking as a profession after reading a magazine article that ranked it near the top of the country's highest-paying careers. "I made a decision to turn toward Wall Street," Tony says. "By twenty-five, I was a hedge fund vice president. I'd hit my goal. And I was like, now what? I felt like there was nowhere else to go."

His doctor suggested some cognitive behavioral therapy for the depression. Tony asked him, "Can I just take a pill?" The psychiatrist said yes, and then asked questions about Tony's ability to focus, something he hadn't really thought about. Tony answered honestly, that it wasn't a problem. But he also mentioned that he had tried Adderall a few times in college and found it fantastic.

"The doctor asked me basically, 'Was the Adderall useful?' And of course it was, it did wonders for my grades. So he said, 'If you want I can start you on a low-dose prescription for that too,' and I thought, sure, why not?"

Tony started taking 10 mg of Adderall a day. (The customary dose starts at 5mg and goes up, only if necessary, at 5mg increments weekly, rarely exceeding 40 mg a day.) Six years later, Tony has a prescribed dose of 90 mg a day. The reason he needs so much now is that he's built up a tolerance to the drug from such long-term use. In fact, he has developed a system of drug use he tells me is "super stable" and reminds me of Peter's system of recording the dosages and timing of injections in order to avoid overdosing. Tony explains: "I compress the dosage for three weeks—so I use 120 mg a day—and then I ease up a little coming to the end of three weeks and don't use for the last week of the month. I can time myself so that I come down on Sunday—I developed an algorithm that lets me optimize the dosage," he explains. "I overdose, so to speak, in the beginning, and then I have a week to chill."

We are sitting at a counter in the window of a midtown coffee shop and Tony is, without a doubt, wired. He's dressed fairly causally—jeans, a button-down shirt, and brightly colored athletic shoes—and is speaking quickly, tapping his foot, whipping out his phone to show me a new app he created and then photos of his dog. Tony is so productive now he is able to complete complex side projects for the firm and for himself in his off-hours. In addition to his VP responsibilities he recently began overseeing information technology at the firm, including managing security, which is extremely important in finance. "I taught myself to penetration-test firewalls," Tony tells me. "I wrote a new app that's proprietary, just for our firm, to manage investments. And I've been tinkering a little with hacking too." Employees in most countries work less as they become wealthier, but highly paid workers in the United States, like Tony, actually work more—later at night, earlier in the morning, and on weekends.

Alexandra Michel, a former Goldman Sachs associate and now a business professor at the University of Pennsylvania, has spent more than a decade researching how working this way transforms employees. She did a nine-year study of investment bankers and found they would allow their physical health to decline in order to be better, higher-achieving investment bankers, some of whom worked up to 120 hours *per week,* even when there was nothing urgent to do.

It might seem reasonable to assume that physicians, of all white-collar professionals, know enough about addiction to steer clear of substance abuse. That could be why the percentage of doctors that will develop a substance-use disorder is about the same as it is for the general population, 10 to 12 percent. But doctors are five times as likely to misuse prescription drugs (as opposed to street drugs), probably because they have easy access to them, and their addiction (when compared with the general public) is usually much more advanced by the time it is identified and treated. The authors of a five-year study of doctors with mental health or substance-use problems found that those in anesthesiology, emergency medicine, and psychiatry were particularly susceptible to addiction. The top three reasons for drug abuse were the same as those cited by other kinds of professionals: to manage physical pain, to manage emotional and psychiatric distress, and to manage stress.

In addition to law, finance, and medicine, the tech industry has a drug problem too. Anne Delaware, an addiction nurse and counselor who has worked in the field for thirty-five years (including intake and counseling positions at musician Eric Clapton's Crossroads Centre in Antigua, which provides high-end addiction treatment), said one of her clients in Silicon Valley recently told her about being in the boardroom of a large technology company and seeing cocaine all over the table. "He said everyone was 'doing lines' and he felt like he had to do it too," she told me. "It's like the 1980s in the Valley now, with all the amphetamine and cocaine use." Delaware also facilitates the multifamily group program at Summit Estate Recovery Center's outpatient facility in Saratoga, California, a small, affluent city in Silicon Valley.

Although I interviewed clinicians at Summit and spoke to patients, I wanted to reach more people in the tech industry to get some sense of how widespread drug use is and what, exactly, people are using. I posted a query to the online discussion forum Hacker News in the summer of 2018, asking users to tell me—using only their HN handles as identification—about their experience of drug use, either directly or what they were seeing around them.

Hacker News is owned by the start-up accelerator Y Combinator in Silicon Valley (it provides seed funding for new businesses and helps guide them through the early stages of development). The Hacker News site gets about four million views a day, and it is used largely by those working in technology and related fields like finance and the hard sciences (where the introduction of new technologies has been transformative). Ten hours after I posted my initial query, I had six hundred responses. I would have had more but many potential commenters posted they were worried about being publicly candid, even if only identified by their user name. I soon got a secure and encrypted email address, which made those who wanted to email me privately more comfortable about doing so.

A large number of commenters wrote that they were using stimulants and marijuana. "I love stims, especially modafinil [modafinil is used to promote wakefulness in people who suffer from extreme sleepiness, a condition known as narcolepsy]," wrote one commenter in response to my post. "I've witnessed time and time again the scenario where person A is completely awestruck by person B and their accomplishments and doesn't realize it's because they have a literal advantage due to performance enhancing drugs. Then someone says, 'Oh yeah, so and so takes a ton of Adderall, didn't you know?' and everything begins to make more sense."

Another HN commenter wrote that he used Adderall and cocaine. "I remember a CEO of one of my early start-ups would give me 5 mg addies to help me get more done. I appreciated it because it was great to get the added boost to focus. I eventually worked my way up to taking 30 mg of XR [extended release] (legally, doctor prescribed) and it was the most productive I have ever been in my life. I worked 24 x 7. I was working a normal consulting job while also working on a start-up/app in my spare time. I did ui/ux/frontend/backend/api development and sent cash overseas for an iOS developer that I managed. None of this would have been possible without stimulants." Yet this engineer also found the lifestyle unsustainable, he wrote, and quit cold turkey, something he didn't recommend. Quitting Adderall all at once can cause serious depression and anxiety, as well as a host of other symptoms, among them nausea, panic attacks, headaches, and vacillation between insomnia and sleeping too much.

Grant, who used to be a senior manager at gamemaker Zynga in San Francisco, told me his opioid addiction began one afternoon at a point in his life when he felt miserable in his job. He Googled "how to find pain pills on the streets of SF." Half an hour later he was walking back to his office with a pocketful of Vicodin, a commonly prescribed opioid painkiller. The pill made him feel better about everything, says Grant, who has a history of depression. But what started out as one 10 mg pill every four or six hours has evolved, five years later, into a 300–400-mg-a-day habit. Grant has spent more than $100,000 over the past five years on drugs.

Others on the forum talked about microdosing LSD, which is just what it sounds like—taking very small amounts of acid. Some commenters said it made them more creative and productive. One user wrote that he has both microdosed LSD and taken small amounts (less than 5 mg) of d-methamphetamine (a drug prescribed under the brand name Desoxyn, used to treat ADHD and obesity). "LSD can certainly increase productivity," he wrote, adding that it also provided a boost of energy similar to what he could get from an amphetamine. In journalist Michael Pollan's 2018 book *How to Change Your Mind* about the history, science, and effects of psychedelics, he writes that "the practice of microdosing—taking a tiny 'subperceptual' regular dose of LSD as a kind of mental tonic—is all the rage in the tech community."

Those who responded to me on HN were using modafinil, Adderall, Ritalin, lots of marijuana, cocaine, and ketamine (an anesthetic drug used illegally as a hallucinogen).

An online discussion ensued about whether or not, as humans, we are evolved for what a career in technology—or for what technology in general—demands. One commenter wrote that those in tech use a variety of these drugs because human beings aren't "built for 8+ hours a day of intense abstract reasoning, which seems to be what the modern information economy demands of those aspiring to a middle class or better existence."

BECAUSE THERE ARE NO comprehensive studies of how chemical substances, legal and illegal, are being used or abused by American professionals, the information we have is largely anecdotal. We do know that for the first time in nearly a decade, cocaine use in the United States is increasing. A 2017 State

Department report noted "troubling early signs that cocaine use and availability is on the rise." In just one year, from 2014 to 2015, there were 766,000 new cocaine users in the country.

We also know, from an analysis of data published in the *American Journal of Public Health* in 2016, that the number of adults who filled a benzodiazepine prescription—sedatives like Xanax and Klonopin—increased almost 70 percent between 1996 and 2013, to 13.5 million prescriptions. To get a broader perspective on the scope of drug use by professionals, I decided to speak with some of the counselors, therapists, and doctors that treat white-collar addiction.

One of them is Mark Stahlhuth, a psychologist who, when I met him, was clinical director of Seasons in Malibu, a residential and outpatient treatment center in Malibu, California, which looks more like a resort than a rehab, situated on a bluff overlooking Matador Beach. The facility treats about 150 clients a year and it's not cheap—a one-month stay (typical for residential treatment) is $59,500 for a shared room and $83,000 for a single. Clients here are generally executives, celebrities, and their adult children between thirty-five and sixty-five years old. Nearly all of them also have a mental health issue like anxiety, depression, or bipolar disorder; 90 percent have had some kind of trauma in their past. The patients at Seasons are largely addicted to alcohol and prescription pills. "Although we see a little meth and cocaine too," said Stahlhuth.

He, like many of the clinicians I spoke with, hears repeatedly from clients that they feel an urgent need to escape from their daily lives. When love is predicated on performance, Stahlhuth says, like how much you earn each year, your title in the firm, or how much business you just brought in, the pressure to perform is enormous. Added to that is the pressure that generally exists in the workplace today to innovate, to keep up with the speed of technology and keep shareholders (many of whom are no longer willing to wait for longer-term earnings) happy. "I see business owners who feel this intense need to create, create, create," said Stahlhuth. "And then innovate, innovate, innovate."

Quest Diagnostics, which provides a wide range of diagnostic testing for health care, does an annual survey of drug use in the American workforce, and in 2018 found drug use to be at its highest rate in more than a decade, driven largely by the surging use of cocaine and amphetamines, as well as marijuana in states where recreational use is legal.

Sam Ball, the psychologist and director of the executives and professionals program at Silver Hill Hospital, says the higher the level of achievement, the more there is to lose, so the higher the level of denial—not only on the part of the addict but also among those around them. "With Peter, some of the people he worked with may have known there was a problem and just looked the other way because they didn't want to get into a big HR issue or liability issues. But a lot of people are just in denial. It's part of the disease's effect—the people closest to the person affected should be able to see what's going on but don't," he said. I certainly didn't.

PSYCHIATRISTS AND PHYSICIANS WHO study addiction have found that somewhere between 40 to 60 percent of a person's susceptibility is genetic. A 2012 paper published in the journal *Psychiatric Clinics of North America* found that "heritability estimates for addictions range between 40 percent (hallucinogens) to 70 percent (cocaine)." According to research from the National Institute on Drug Abuse (NIDA), both genetics and the environment conspire to create addiction problems, and that means there isn't one simple reason why a person becomes an addict or an alcoholic. Some people are just at higher risk for the disease. When I take a Vicodin, I vomit; when Peter took one, he felt fantastic. Those responses are biological, they have nothing to do with moral fiber or strength of character or anything else.

Beverly Roesch, a therapist and clinical director at Cirque Lodge, a high-end treatment facility in the mountains of Sundance, Utah, says one significant environmental factor among people at the upper end of the socioeconomic spectrum is a profound lack of "intrinsic spirituality," at least in the clients she has seen over the years. Not religion, not even belief in a god of some kind, but a longing for some bigger meaning in their lives, a feeling of being connected to something larger than what's in front of them. "This is a deficit that all the money and all the trappings do not address," Roesch tells me. "What they are missing is connection to others, a sense of community."

I asked Judson Brewer, a psychiatrist who specializes in addiction and studies how mindfulness practices affect the brain, for his thoughts on the professionals he treats. When we met, Brewer was division chief of the Center for Mindfulness at the University of Massachusetts Medical School. He is now director of research and innovation at Brown University's Mindfulness Center. Brewer's own experience with major depression, later diagnosed as bipolar disorder, gives him some understanding of why people seek relief for their disquiet and distress through mood-altering substances.

We sat in his bright office with windows overlooking the woods behind the center. Brewer, who treats both low- and high-income addiction patients, said Peter's case highlights something clinicians should know but many still seem to be learning. "Being intelligent and very fluent is not a protection against addiction. In fact, in some cases it can be enabling because you feel you know better, that you'll never become prey to this. And being well-off means you have access, essentially unlimited access, to drugs. Someone like this will start out saying, 'This is just a pill. I've got it under control,'" said Brewer. "Until, of course, they don't."

■ FOURTEEN

Better Living Through Chemistry

TWO GENERATIONS ARE NOW preparing for, or beginning, their own white-collar futures—Millennials and Gen Z. In 2020, this group spans from eight-year-olds (the youngest Gen Zs) to thirty-nine-year-olds (the oldest Millennials). The Pew Research Center defines these generations as having been born between 1981 and 2012, and from this group will come America's future lawyers, legislators, doctors, business owners, CEOs, inventors, scientists, and technologists. Millennials and Gen Z comprise almost half of the U.S. population today. More than one in three—35 percent—of the workforce are Millennials, according to Pew. Right behind them are the oldest members of Gen Z, who are just beginning their careers; today they make up 5 percent of the workforce.

Gen Z (born 1997–2012) is unique in that it is the first generation to have been born into a world where the internet is a significant part of everyday life. Research led by Suniya S. Luthar, a psychology professor at Arizona State University whose work has focused on vulnerability and resilience in young people, found that many teenagers likely destined for white-collar lives already have high levels of substance abuse, anxiety, and depression. In a 2013 paper, Luthar and two colleagues wrote that "upper-middle-class youth, who are en route to the most prestigious universities and well-paying careers in America, are more likely to be more troubled than their middle-class counterparts. Youth in poverty are widely recognized as being 'at risk,' but increasingly, significant problems have been seen at the other end of the socioeconomic continuum."

Luthar began to sense something counterintuitive happening in the mid-1990s, almost incidentally, while studying inner-city teens. A comparison group of affluent students had also been recruited for her study, but this comparison group had significantly higher rates of substance use than their lower socioeconomic counterparts, including cigarettes, alcohol, marijuana, and "hard drugs." A decade later the findings were replicated in a study of suburban tenth graders.

In 2017, according to the University of Michigan's annual *Monitoring the Future* study, marijuana use among adolescents was up for the first time in seven years. In the 2018 survey, nearly 28 percent of tenth graders and 36 percent of twelfth graders said they regularly use it. (By the time the youngest Gen Zs are in the workforce, marijuana could be legal for recreational use in a majority of states.)

Substance use and abuse increases as well-off high school graduates head to college, says Luthar. "Every single school we looked at—public, private, day schools, boarding schools, East and West Coast, South, Midwest, every single one of them—we've seen this pattern, high levels of substance abuse or high rates of depression and anxiety. The common denominator, without exception, was that the school was a 'high-achieving' school."

Although this book is focused on drug use and abuse at the upper end of the income curve, those at the lower end have been enormously impacted by drug addiction of all kinds. Heroin addiction, for example, is more than three times as common in those who earn less than $20,000 a year compared to those earning more than $50,000 a year, according to the CDC. Heroin addicts with either no insurance or Medicaid vastly outnumber those with private health insurance, and that severely limits their access to treatment—let alone good, comprehensive treatment—for the disease. Poverty and substance use often operate hand-in-hand, and research going back to at least the early 1990s has shown that neighborhoods with poor housing conditions, higher levels of school dropouts, unemployment, and single-parent families have higher levels of drug use. There has been far less research done into drug use among adolescents from well-off families, and Luthar wanted to learn more about them.

She and her researchers followed a group of upper-middle-class students in high-achieving high schools through college until they were twenty-seven. By age twenty-six, almost 40 percent of the young men and 25 percent of the women had a diagnosis of addiction, two to three times the usual rate for people this age. "Not abuse," Luthar emphasizes. "Addiction." And the earlier in their lives kids start to use, the more likely they are to abuse as adults and the more difficult it will be for them to quit.

Anxiety may be one reason why they are developing drug problems. It has surpassed depression as the reason college students most often seek out counseling services. According to the 2018 annual report from the Center for Collegiate Mental Health at Penn State University and data from the National College Health Assessment, about half of college students suffer from depression. In the previous year, more than 63 percent reported feeling overwhelming anxiety; about one in twelve had made a suicide plan.

Many factors contribute to anxiety and depression, but among the most profound differences between Gen Z and any other generation in history is that Gen Z hasn't known a world without social media. As these children get older, the pressure they feel to achieve in all aspects of their lives can be intensified by social media. Luthar is concerned about the lack of genuine connection with others many of these young people feel. "This hooking up (casual sexual encounters) and not being able to have real, interpersonal relationships because there's no time in their jam-packed schedules," she says. "Instead they use Instagram and Snapchat." And those are no substitute for real intimacy—physical and emotional—with another person.

Jean M. Twenge, a professor of psychology at San Diego State University who studies and writes about generational differences, started seeing a pattern of rising mental health issues for adolescents beginning in 2012, especially anxiety, depression, and loneliness. At first, she thought these might be statistical blips of some sort, but they persisted in other national surveys too.

Eventually she determined what was significant about the year 2012. It was the moment in history when the proportion of Americans who owned a smartphone exceeded 50 percent. By 2015, according to Twenge, 92 percent of teens and young adults owned one. "Thus," wrote Twenge and her co-authors in a research paper, "smartphones were used by the majority of teens the year that depressive symptoms began to increase and by nearly all teens when depressive symptoms peaked. Another study found major depressive episodes among teens ages 12 to 17 increased beginning in 2011."

Millennials grew up as the web grew up, but it wasn't in their lives around the clock; when Gen Z came into the world the web had already transformed it. Smartphones existed, albeit mostly in the form of the BlackBerry, until 2007, when Apple unveiled its first iPhone. That year the oldest Gen Zs were eleven. "The arrival of the smartphone has radically changed every aspect of teenagers' lives, from the nature of their social interactions to their mental health," Twenge has written. "These changes have affected young people in every corner of the nation and in every type of household. The trends appear among teens poor and rich; of every ethnic background; in cities, suburbs, and small towns. Where there are cell towers, there are teens living their lives on their smartphone." Today, the average age at which a child gets their first phone is 10.3, and nearly 40 percent of children have access to the web via their phones.

It's not just the phone, of course, but the world to which it grants access. Social media is now a part of children's lives long before most of them hit puberty. Nearly 40 percent establish their first social media account—be it Facebook, Instagram, Twitter, or Snapchat—before they are twelve.

This has fundamentally changed the way people interact with one another. A 2018 research report found that 65 percent of people under 35 in the United States communicate more digitally than they do in person; in the United Kingdom, it's 74 percent. Yet words alone account for only a fraction of our understanding of what someone is trying to tell us; there is so much more that goes into communicating with another person. Albert Mehrabian, a professor emeritus of psychology at UCLA well known for his research into verbal and nonverbal communication, found that a person's tone of voice alone accounts for about 40 percent of communication; body language accounts for 55 percent. In order to meaningfully convey to someone else how we are feeling or what we are thinking, these three components—words, tone of voice, and body language—need to be working together. That doesn't happen in a text message.

In a Pew Research Center survey, teenagers said they are trying to cut back on phone and social media use. It won't be easy. Phones were designed to be addictive. They operate on a principle known as variable interval reinforcement, developed by the behavioral psychologist B. F. Skinner. Here's how it works: A behavior—pulling a lever on a slot machine, scratching numbers off a lottery ticket, or checking your phone—is reinforced intermittently and randomly by a reward. With your phone, the reward is a new text or a notification from an app (like Tinder, for example, or a "like" on your last Instagram post). Your brain is seeking the reward but doesn't know when it will happen, which makes you that much more determined to keep at it. "Part of what makes slot machines so alluring is the promise of maybe at some point hitting the jackpot. And we end up spending huge amounts of time seeking out that kind of reward," says Adam Alter, an associate professor of marketing at New York University's Stern School of Business and the author of *Irresistible: The Rise of Addictive Technology and the Business of Keeping Us Hooked.* "If you buy lottery tickets or scratch cards it's nice to win, but it's really that feeling when you're about to start playing, that buzz you get from wondering whether this is the time you're going to win. That is really addictive to people."

GEN Z AND MILLENNIALS are unique in another way too. Many have grown up using medication to help them manage mental health problems such as depression, anxiety, and ADHD. In her book, *Dosed: The Medication Generation Grows Up,* Kaitlin Bell Barnett examined the psychological impact of having grown up on psychoactive medications like the antidepressant Prozac, which she began taking at seventeen. Barnett, who is an older Millennial—she was just shy of twenty-nine when her book was published in 2012—wrote, "For the first time in history, millions of young Americans have grown up taking psychotropic medications that have shaped their experiences and relationships, their emotions and personalities, and perhaps most fundamentally, their very sense of themselves."

Long-term use of antidepressants is increasing in the United States. A 2018 analysis of federal data by *The New York Times* found that about 15.5 million Americans have been taking antidepressants for at least five years; that rate has doubled since 2010, and more than tripled since 2000. And a study published in December 2017 in the journal *Psychiatric Services* found that the use of antidepressants for children and adolescents has come back to the level it was before 2004, when prescribing for youth declined because of an FDA warning about heightened suicide risk.

Many of the psychiatrists I spoke to for this book are concerned that parents often want medications to help their children with problems that aren't really disorders, like boredom, daydreaming, or misbehaving in school. Journalist Katherine Sharpe wrote about the potential emotional and psychological costs of long-term use of antidepressants and other medications in her book, *Coming of Age on Zoloft*. Sharpe, who started taking the antidepressant Zoloft when she was eighteen, wrote in an essay in *The Wall Street Journal* that drugs "undoubtedly help many young people who are genuinely struggling. But the expanding use of psychiatric medication in youth over the last twenty years has meant that the drugs are now prescribed in less and less severe cases."

In 1980, the *Diagnostic and Statistical Manual of Mental Disorders, Third Edition*, introduced the category of ADD—attention deficit disorder, either with or without hyperactivity. In 1987 it was replaced by attention deficit/hyperactivity disorder, or ADHD, today the most common childhood behavioral health problem leading to medical and behavioral interventions. According to the

CDC, about 11 percent of American children age 4–17 have received a diagnosis.

The disorder is treated with stimulants, the most well-known among them being Adderall, which came on the market in 1996. There were 91 million prescriptions for ADHD drugs worldwide in 2017, according to an industry report from market research firm IBISWorld, and adults recently overtook children in terms of their share of that market. It's estimated that as much as 35 percent of college students use ADHD medication without a prescription, and there is usually a supply of it "on any given dorm floor at any time," write Stephen P. Hinshaw and Richard M. Scheffler in their book *The ADHD Explosion*.

Few people in the world know more about ADHD than Hinshaw, a clinical psychologist and psychology professor at the University of California, Berkeley, and a psychiatry professor and vice-chair for child and adolescent psychology at the University of California, San Francisco. I asked him if he thinks we are seeing the emergence of a generation dependent on stimulants. "That's the sixty-four-zillion-dollar question, isn't it?" he says. "Part of the increased use of these medications is the legitimate recognition of a disorder. However, the skyrocketing rates of increase go beyond recognition of a condition—unless there is an epidemic, and ADHD isn't contagious."

Hinshaw says the vast majority of pediatricians diagnose the disorder "in twelve minutes." ADHD is diagnosed based on a set of symptoms; there is no blood test or brain scan to confirm its existence. "If you want a formula for creating unacceptably high rates of diagnoses, incentivize academic performance in kids above all else and make sure that standards for assessing and diagnosing ADHD are lax," says Hinshaw.

Young children may be misdiagnosed, but they rarely fake ADHD symptoms; adults, however, often do—about one in four, according to several studies, including a well-cited one published in 2010 in the journal *The Clinical Neuropsychologist*. Many of the adults in the study that faked symptoms wanted medication because they were having a tough time dealing with their workloads and their lives. "A lot of people think they have it because they are struggling, but it's not because of ADHD," said the study's lead author, clinical neuropsychologist Paul Marshall, in an interview. "Oftentimes, it's simply depression, anxiety, or lack of sleep."

Hinshaw and his research team have been following and interviewing hundreds of people with and without ADHD about their drug use and mental health over the past two decades. (Hinshaw says other research teams have followed even larger groups.) For those without ADHD, he says, "We hear over and over again, 'I feel like I'm a better person when I'm on these drugs.'"

IT'S A TUESDAY NIGHT in March 2018, and I am at the Williamsburg Hotel in Brooklyn, speaking to a private gathering of the NYC Salon, a speaker series started a few years ago by two Millennials, Tarun Chitra, who left graduate school (he was studying theoretical physics at Cornell) to work on creating artificial intelligence software used by finance companies, and Ruth Nachmany, a software engineer at Warby Parker, an online retailer of prescription glasses. They started inviting people with novel insights or interesting projects in art, economics, science, technology, and comedy to give talks about their work and process. The group got so large (more than 3,000 members, according to NYC Salon's Facebook page) it had to be closed to new members. Meetings occur every other Tuesday night at different locations.

About thirty-five young men and women are here to listen to me speak about my research for this book and to talk to me about drug use, both their own and in their social circles. I have agreed not to use people's names or identify the companies for which they work. One man in his late twenties who has his own tech company tells me he popped an Adderall right before this event. "It's been a long day and I needed something to help stay focused," he explains. A woman sitting next to him turns to me and elaborates. "It's not like it's an escape. It's coping," she says. "You'd be surprised how many people are still riding off the Adderall high they have been riding all day long, and you've just never seen them in their natural state."

I make my way over to the next group. A man in a gray sweater introduces himself. "I'm twenty-nine and I worked in finance out of college and now I'm in med school. I worked for many years in investment banking, researching pharma companies. I've used drugs my entire life. Weed and MDMA [also known as ecstasy or Molly, a stimulant and hallucinogen] in college. When I started working I did stimulants on and off prescription. I bought some today, actually. It's all about the risk-benefit ratio, and the benefits for me outweigh the risks," he says. "The human brain didn't evolve to be staring at numbers all the time. I think part of the reason we use drugs in cognitively demanding fields is because humans haven't been able to evolve fast enough to meet the demands of modern society." I think he may be onto something.

The use of stimulants to enhance memory, concentration, and overall performance increased 180 percent, on average, from 2015 to 2017, in fifteen countries that took part in the Global Drug Survey, an online survey that has collected data from more than 100,000 people. The United States had the highest rates of stimulant use both years.

Many of the people in this room use the drug ketamine for partying (they call it Special K). It's actually an anesthetic (used, for example, in hospitals and on the battlefield) but at low doses produces hallucinations and mood changes, and can make users feel dissociated both from their body and reality. (Research shows ketamine may be effective in treating depression that isn't responding to other treatments. In March 2019, the FDA approved a new drug from Johnson & Johnson based on ketamine that is administered via a nasal spray.)

Two other drugs mentioned frequently tonight are modafinil (the stimulant that treats narcolepsy) and LSD, used in very small doses. A thirty-year-old physician tells me he regularly microdoses LSD and uses Adderall and small amounts of fentanyl too. "Look, a doctor's job is to give medication to patients, so we are very good at dosing medication," he says, adding that he often doses himself while working. I ask if he feels at all ethically compromised, treating patients after he has taken medication himself. "Doctors can get overconfident, of course. I have a hard line against benzos and opiates. I do enjoy them but I also know they are very addictive. I had an attending [physician] that died last month from an opiate overdose. He was using alcohol and benzos and opiates."

WHAT DOES ALL THIS mean for the future? I'm not sure. I wanted to learn more about what was driving drug use and abuse among some of the most privileged people in America. What I have found is that the reasons people use are complicated and individual, and there is rarely just one reason. Peter's personal history and the culture and time in which he lived, the profession he chose, his genetics and personality, all of it in all of its complexity informed his decision to start down a road he likely thought of as a way to chemically enhance his life. Or chemically escape it. It's too late for me or anyone else to help him see that it would not lead to feeling better, that it would not solve his problems. I can, however, sound a warning for those who may inadvertently follow in his footsteps. Right now, some of the youngest members of society are involved in a giant chemistry experiment, the results of which have yet to be seen.

It's unclear how the brain's prefrontal cortex—which is involved in planning, attention, problem-solving, error-monitoring, and decision-making—will be affected by exposure to the doses of amphetamines used by many college and high school students.

In a 2017 article on psychostimulants, researchers at Children's Hospital of Philadelphia and Drexel University College of Medicine wrote that the drive for cognitive enhancement is unlikely to decrease, and they expressed concern that the lack of knowledge about what happens to children and adolescents using psychostimulants like Adderall "may be perpetuating a perception of these drugs as 'safe' for any age when that might not be true."

And what about the use of marijuana? A recent Gallup poll found that one in four young adults under thirty now uses it on a regular or occasional basis. There are very few studies of cannabis use during adolescence, a time when the brain may be particularly vulnerable to the effects of THC (tetrahydrocannabinol, the ingredient in marijuana that makes a user feel high). A study published in *The Journal of Neuroscience* in January 2019 found that the brains of adolescents who smoked one or two joints before they were fourteen had more gray matter than teens who didn't use marijuana. The increase was seen mostly in the amygdala, an area of the brain that processes emotions, and the hippocampus, which affects memory development and spatial abilities.

What this might mean isn't clear yet, but one of the study's lead authors, University of Vermont psychiatry professor Hugh Garavan, said that at around age fourteen the adolescent brain is typically undergoing a pruning process, where it (that gray matter) gets *thinner*—not thicker—as it refines its synaptic connections. The teens using marijuana, he said, may be disrupting that process.

Judith Grisel, a psychology professor at Bucknell University and author of *Never Enough: The Neuroscience and Experience of Addiction,* says marijuana "can change the course of brain development and have long-lasting effects on brain pathways having to do with mood and cognition and susceptibility to addiction." Cannabis use also appears to increase—rather than decrease, as is commonly assumed—the risk of misusing and overusing prescription opioids.

Sam Ball, the addiction psychologist, is deeply concerned about adolescents using marijuana. "If you take the developing adolescent brain and what may be a fully accessible drug, the rates of kids starting to smoke pot at twelve or thirteen will absolutely go up," he says. "And you're not going to have overdose deaths like you do now—maybe some drug-driving fatalities, but you aren't going to have 70,000 people die of an overdose of marijuana in a year. You will, however, see the more insidious effects over the course of this adolescent's development. It will impair their schoolwork, family relationships, work functioning. And some people will become psychotic. I think it is going to grow as a problem much more quietly than opioids, but it will be far-reaching," he says.

Beverly Roesch, the addiction therapist at Cirque Lodge, told me the treatment center sees many clients who used a lot of marijuana and kicked off a psychotic disorder (like schizophrenia). "If you're predisposed to a psychotic illness, marijuana fast-tracks you to it," she says. "It may have medicinal value, but it is also a powerful psychoactive agent." And it's more powerful than it has ever been. An analysis of marijuana samples seized during drug busts from 1995 to 2014 showed THC concentrations increased from about 4 percent in 1995 to 12 percent in 2014. Three years later, in 2017, *High Times* magazine ranked the twelve strongest cannabis strains in the world. The top four had a THC content of more than 30 percent—that's more than seven times as strong as marijuana was in 1995. Long-term use is also associated with health and psychiatric problems later in life, cognitive difficulties, and lifetime alcohol problems.

If these drugs aren't safe but are used for decades, I wonder what these kids will be like when they are thirty or forty or fifty. Will their maturity be delayed because of how the drugs affected their prefrontal cortex? Will it impact their decision-making ability, reasoning, memory? If people under thirty become dependent on amphetamines and other stimulants, cannabis and tiny doses of acid to cope with the productivity and creative problem-solving requirements of their professions, what drugs will they require to cope with the rest of their lives?

After all the research I've done about addiction, all the studies and books I've read, all the experts I've interviewed, this question remains. Are we coping with the difficult parts of life by distracting ourselves with addictions—to our phones, streaming video, work, food, porn, news, shopping, drugs? Many of the people I spoke with about their current or past drug use said they felt disconnected and lonely. In 2000, Facebook didn't even exist; today it is the largest and perhaps loneliest "community" in the world.

Harvard professor and political scientist Robert Putnam, in his 2000 book *Bowling Alone,* chronicled that growing feeling of isolation in writing about the decline of American communities. According to the 2018 American Time Use Survey, people in the United States spend about thirty-eight minutes a day socializing and communicating—face-to-face—with others.

The world around us may be changing dramatically, but I believe our needs as human beings aren't. A series of studies done back in 1993 found that when a person's central aspirations are "self-acceptance, affiliation and community feeling" they feel less distress in life and more well-being. It's as if the digital age has made us think of human connection and support as more an option than a necessity. Yet isn't it critically important to feel truly—not virtually—connected to something bigger than ourselves, even if that something is just our neighbors? "It's in relationships that we find recovery," Dan Lukasik, the founder of Lawyers With Depression, told me. "We can be damaged by relationships, but we are also resurrected by them."

Sam Quinones, the author of *Dreamland: The True Tale of America's Opiate Epidemic,* perhaps the definitive book on the evolution of the opioid crisis, testified before Congress in January 2018, answering questions and giving his thoughts on how the crisis might be addressed. At the end of his testimony, Quinones said, "This scourge is about issues far deeper than drug addiction. It's about isolation, [the] hollowing out of small-town America and the middle class, of the silo-ization of our society, and it's about a culture that acts as if buying stuff is the path to happiness. This epidemic shows us no matter how high the stock market rises, how rich some Americans have grown, that neither we, nor they, can isolate ourselves from the world. Problems will find them, and us. I believe therefore that the antidote to heroin is not naloxone. It is community. Community is the response to a scourge rooted in our own isolation."

But building a social support system—a brick-and-mortar one, not a virtual one—takes time. It takes more time and effort to call someone and have a conversation with them, or make plans to see them and execute those plans, than it does to send a text. And likewise, it's easier to take a pill or buy something new to make sadness or anxiety disappear or, at least, distract us from it, rather than just sitting still and actually processing what is going on in our lives. That is difficult. I know. Like so many others I struggle each day to resist the temptations that invite me, at every turn, to distract myself. For better or worse, I am part of a consumption-fueled society that keeps seeking what it thinks will finally make it feel okay: more.

Psychiatrist Judson Brewer told me, "People like Peter think, 'just this much more and then I'll be happy.' But it will never be enough. The problem is that we are not comfortable with ourselves, with being ourselves. And we can't bear to spend ten minutes with that discomfort," he says. "That's why we're always looking for something else."

PART IV

■ FIFTEEN
April 2018

EVAN AND I ARE in Ann Arbor, Michigan, to attend Anna's college graduation tomorrow. It is nearly six P.M. and all the restaurants in town are overflowing with visiting families. We decide to make dinner at Anna's apartment: risotto with chicken, asparagus, and peas. I pour chicken broth into a large pot and start heating it while Evan chops up shallots and garlic, adding them to a pan of rice, olive oil, and white wine. Next to him I sauté small pieces of chicken. Anna connects her phone to speakers in the living room and starts flipping through playlists on Spotify to find a song she wants us to hear.

Her roommate is in and out, packing up and getting ready to move on, both physically and metaphorically. I look around the apartment as I cook, at the IKEA throw pillows, the string of lights carefully positioned over an Indian-print wall hanging, the collection of burned and beat-up pots and pans in the kitchen, the mismatched mugs and glasses—many sporting the school's signature slogans, *Go Blue* and *Hail.* She will miss this, I think. The late nights hanging out with her roommate, talking boys and friends and politics and the future. Pregames, sorority date parties, hungover breakfasts, the red Solo cups scattered on frat house lawns, your best friends just around the corner, all of it.

After dinner, Evan and I head to the Ann Arbor Regent Hotel. I'm not sure how I originally found this place, but it is where Peter, Evan, and I stayed during move-in weekend four years ago. We were on the first floor then; this weekend we're on the second, at the opposite end of the hotel. Late on Friday night I leave the room to get a cup of tea from the little dining area downstairs. The hotel is quiet, which makes sense, as graduation is early tomorrow morning. It looks exactly the same as it did the first time we stayed here. I lift the lid of my paper cup to blow on the tea, trying to cool it, then walk down the hallway looking for the rooms we had four years ago. I stand in front of the one I think I shared with Evan. Several feet farther down is the one where Peter stayed. I don't know what I'm hoping for, other than to remember how it felt to be here then, the four of us together for the weekend.

I walk down to the room I think was Peter's and remember packing up the things he left behind as he rushed home to San Diego. Back then I accepted his explanation, that it was a work crisis; now I know better.

I'm trying hard to remember if I saw any hint of what was to come, if there was something that didn't seem obvious but should have. In his room, when we packed up, I don't recall any signs— not one tiny round Band-Aid or individually packaged alcohol wipe. I didn't see any orange pill vials or sterile syringes in their slim paper wrapping—those would certainly have raised some questions. I had never even seen a single-use sterile syringe up close until Peter's death. I thought of them only in the context of medical labs and blood work and pediatricians' offices. Now I know more than I ever imagined I would (only I never imagined such a thing). The Luer Lock tip, the calibration marks, the plunger that fits inside the barrel (which has a kind of collar on one end to keep the syringe from slipping during injections). The sharp metal needle with its beveled tip and heel at one end and little hub at the other, used for attaching it to the syringe. Such a smart little device.

I'm still standing in front of the door when I realize I can hear people inside. I'm not even sure this was actually Peter's room but it doesn't really matter, because whether or not it was his room back then it certainly isn't now. My feelings are complicated, both sad for him and still angry at him. He should be here with us this weekend.

The next morning Evan and I wait with the other parents and siblings of soon-to-be-graduates for the hotel's shuttle to The Big House, Michigan's stadium. It is wickedly cold for late April— barely forty degrees with a driving wind and intermittent, stinging rain. Everyone is dressed as if they are going to a football game. Evan and I follow the crowd onto the bus and it inches its way toward the stadium.

I buy Anna some flowers (yellow roses with a blue ribbon, to match the university's colors), while other parents snap up blankets, hoodies, mittens, and hats to brace themselves for the next two hours. Evan and I find our seats, which would be terrific if this were actually a football game: section 21, row 1. The field is a sea of white chairs, rows and rows of them, and in each one a black-robed-and-capped undergrad. They are a restless, celebratory bunch.

We strain to see Anna but she's on the opposite side of the field, so Evan texts her, asking if she can come over to us for a hug and a couple of photos before the ceremony begins. She is heading our way with a friend and we start waving to them. Seeing

Anna, her right hand holding on to her graduation cap in the wind, laughing, her long wavy hair falling down her back and around her face, I start to cry. I'm so overcome with pride and love, amazed that she did this after all that happened. Just look at her, I'm thinking. She graduated on time, even achieving honors in her major. "Hey, sweetie!" I say as she climbs up into our row. We hug one another, the three of us in a tight little circle.

"Mom, don't cry," Anna says gently, and Evan pats my back. "I'm just, I'm so emotional all of a sudden," I say, wiping the tears. The other truth, of course, is that Peter's absence today is so palpable it's a presence. He's not here, but at times like this he's everywhere, almost more powerful in death than he was in life. It's been almost three years that he's been gone and yet I still catch myself sometimes, watching for him.

There are a host of speakers listed in the program, students and faculty, and then the commencement speaker, Michigan alumnus and former NFL player (and Heisman Trophy winner) Charles Woodson.

Woodson starts by talking about his glory days on the university's football team, about running down the sideline during some big game. Two-thirds of the way through the speech he shifts focus and begins talking about the kind of person each graduate should strive to be—a person who is able to ask for help and give help when needed. He is quoting martial artist Bruce Lee, who once described his own psychological and spiritual awakening as the ability to be like water. "Be like water making its way through cracks," Woodson is saying, quoting Lee. "Adjust to the object and you shall find your way around it or through it. Be formless, shapeless, like water. If you put water into a cup, it becomes that cup. If you put water into a bottle, it becomes that bottle. You put water into a teapot, it becomes that teapot. Water can flow or it can crash. Be water, my friend."

Those words are actually Bruce Lee's interpretation of a poem by Chinese philosopher Lao-Tzu, recorded in the 2,600-year-old text known as the *Tao Te Ching (The Book of the Way and Its Virtues)*. There are many translations, but they all more or less amount to this:

The supreme goodness is like water.
It benefits all things without contention.
In dwelling, it stays grounded.
In being, it flows to depths.
In expression, it is honest.
In confrontation, it stays gentle.
In governance, it does not control.
In action, it aligns to timing.
It is content with its nature,
And therefore cannot be faulted.

Perhaps Woodson, standing atop the makeshift stage in the end zone, addressing this crowd of 30,000-some-odd people, is suggesting this ancient Chinese poem could provide some guidance about how to live in our modern, technologically connected, and often emotionally disconnected society.

This is the world my daughter and her peers will now navigate as adults, one that is often intense and chaotic, that moves so fast it can be difficult to figure out where fulfillment lies. I know my daughter will be subject to the pressures, competition, temptations, unpredictability, and tedium that come with adult life. But she will also have to deal with things I never imagined at her age: twenty-four-hour-a-day connectivity, a dual existence (where real life competes with curated social media life), a consumptive society that often prizes—and longs for—celebrity. Her generation's reality seems to me both dystopian and aspirational. They are well aware that this world is one of rising temperatures, heightened sea levels, and vanishing species, a world with too much homelessness and poverty. Yet they also clamor for purpose-driven work, believe dialogue is the way to solve conflicts, and that community is important. They are pragmatic and they are hopeful.

The lesson I take from that Lao-Tzu poem is to be open to change. He used water as an example because, depending on the temperature, it can be a liquid, solid, or gas. That ability to adapt is why water endures, despite an ever-changing environment. I hear Woodson encouraging these new grads to be adaptable in the same way, to go out into the world with confidence but also humility, to seek harmony, not conflict. I want to believe that my daughter and the other graduates in this stadium will do just that, stake out the high ground, think about the problems facing the world and resist the temptation of easy fixes. But I am also afraid for them. Are they prepared to do the hard work required to find satisfaction and contentment in life? To deal, without the help of a pill or powder or pot, with life's difficulties? Will they be able to slow down and find space to think and breathe, to love and truly *live* their lives?

We often make excuses for the addictions and overdoses of superstars—the Philip Seymour Hoffmans, Scott Weilands, and, yes, the more ordinary superstars, the Peters of the world. How else to make sense of their choice to leave extraordinarily fortunate lives for a better high? Judy Chicurel, in a heart-wrenching essay she published in *The New York Times* about her son's drug addiction, asked, "What if you don't possess some superlative talent, if you're not the greatest drummer or photographer or playwright who ever lived? What if you're just a boy who's known setbacks and heartbreak and fear of what lies ahead?" This is at the heart of my concern for all our children. Life is not easy, and life, as Chicurel wrote, "what happens, what you experience, what you choose to take in and decide to leave behind," is the real gateway drug. Our children will need to be nimble, brave, and strong. I scan the field and take in these graduates, laughing with one another, balloons tied to their chairs, sweet messages to their parents written on the flat tops of their caps, and I hope with all my heart they will be.

There is a roar of applause as Woodson leaves the stage. And then it's over and a few minutes later Anna is beside me, smiling, holding bouquets of roses, and posing for photos with her brother, who is beaming at her. As hazy sunlight peeks through the clouds, everything feels okay. I hand my phone to a friend's daughter and ask if she will take a photo of us. Evan and I stand on either side of Anna, our arms around her, and we smile for the camera—big authentic smiles. We are here, the three of us. We are alive and happy and together. Whatever the future holds, for this, I am grateful.

■ AUTHOR'S NOTE

THE STORY YOU HAVE just read is entirely true, based on my best recollection of events and conversations. Although many of the names used are real, others are pseudonyms requested by sources and others who did not want their identities revealed, or whose identities I chose to protect. In one instance I compressed events and created a composite character, done both in service of the narrative and to protect the privacy of several people.

■ ACKNOWLEDGMENTS

LIKE A LOT OF other writers, I always read the acknowledgments. And I always wind up thinking: How can it require so many people—and so much gratitude—to write one book? Now I know the answer. This book exists today because of far more than my efforts.

I am crazy lucky to have the extraordinary Kate Medina as my editor, the talented Erica Gonzalez as assistant editor, and a terrific team supporting me and this book at Random House. I am also indebted to my brilliant, generous agent at WME, Tina Bennett. The collective talents, intelligence, and kindness of these women left me pinching myself most days, unable to believe my good fortune.

The seed for this memoir was planted the day I was given the green light by Phyllis Korkki, my editor at *The New York Times* in 2016, to write the story "The Lawyer, the Addict" for the paper's Sunday business section. When I needed to delay its completion so that I could focus on probate and helping my kids, Phyllis waited for me, all along providing encouragement and guidance. I'm proud to say that that story, which appeared in the *Times* in July 2017, started a long overdue conversation in the legal profession about substance abuse and mental health.

Thanks to my friend William O'Nell for talking me down from the ledge a few days before that story ran, and for everything else you did for me and my children after Peter died, which includes so much it could be a book on its own.

Thank you to Adrienne Brodeur, whom I met in a fiction-writing workshop in San Diego almost thirty years ago and have been following around ever since. Never did I imagine we would both be writing the stories of our lives at the very same time. But if not for our walks up and down Riverside Drive talking about our writing, our families, and our fears, I don't know how I would have seen this through.

Many of the people—especially the women—mentioned in this book comprise part of a core group of friends I made decades ago and who have sustained me (and continue to do so) through the ups and downs of life. They are Jennifer Coburn, an early reader of this book and someone who makes me laugh when I most need it; Edit Zelkind, who helped me understand and correctly define complex medical terminology and ideas; Deirdre O'Shea, who provided incisive editorial feedback; and Irina Shalomayeva, Gary Swedback, Sabine Steck, Larry Tift, Joan and Steve Isaacson, Lisa and Gary Lavin, Linda Braun Leibowitz and David Leibowitz, Tana Slomowitz, Bette Brownlee, Janet Saidi, Ruth Gallant, Lauren and Dan Corcoran, Sandra Parisi, Alison and Joe Cattelona, Lisa Milos, Helen Karagiozis, Diane Wehner, Carol Coburn, and John and Dina Sarbanes. Thanks to each of you for enriching my life and my writing in so many ways.

Thanks to my mom, Charlotte Zimmerman, and my sister,

Judi Quinn, both of whom let me vent early on and kept my confidences; to the world's greatest aunt, Phyllis Schutzman, whose wise and witty emails comforted me during some very dark days; and to the extended family I leaned on: Susan Schutzman, Richard Zimmerman, Flora Haus, and Sherri and Bruce Dunlap. My love and gratitude to Denny Stone, a dear friend whose wise counsel I sought frequently.

In addition to my editors at *The New York Times*, I am grateful to my longtime writing and editing colleagues Joanne Chen, Elaine Pofeldt, Clara Germani, and Ron Donoho for their thoughtful conversations and encouragement; also to Reuben Stern of the University of Missouri School of Journalism for his valuable input. Thank you to the scientists, researchers, teachers, addiction counselors, therapists, psychiatrists, and other professionals who gave so generously of their time in speaking with me and who taught me about the brain, drugs, addiction, consumption, longing, suffering, and . . . well . . . humanity. Thank you to all the people who wrote to me, spoke to me by phone, had coffee with me, and provided their insights and often heartbreaking stories, and to everyone who posted in response to my queries on Hacker News and TopLawSchools.com. I am indebted to each of you for your courage and candor.

The first time I publicly told the story of what happened to Peter was at a storytelling showcase in San Diego known as VAMP, put on monthly by the local nonprofit So Say We All. I was scared to death that night to tell my truth, but afterward felt only relief and liberation, and that experience gave me the courage to keep telling it. Thanks also to the folks at Aspen Summer Words, where I got the chance, in June 2017, to work on the outline of this book with a group of talented writers.

Finally, thank you to my children, for being the awe-inspiring human beings that you are. There were so many times in the last several years when I woke up feeling as if I couldn't face another day, when I questioned what the point of everything was, when I wanted to just pull down the blinds, block out the mess of the world, and sleep for a very long time. I didn't though, because of you two. You are the point of everything.

■ NOTES

PART I

CHAPTER 1: APRIL 1987

8 **"the impacts of adoption"** Child Welfare Information Gateway, "Impact of Adoption on Adopted Persons," August 2013. Retrieved from: https://www.childwelfare.gov/pubs/f_adimpact/.

25 **"has a significant effect"** Linda Nielsen, a professor at Wake Forest University, quoted in Alysse Elhage's June 15, 2015, article, "The Surprising Ways Your Father Impacts Who You'll Marry," in *Verily* magazine.

Ali, Ahmad A., and Daoud, Fawzi S. "Early Father-Daughter Relationship and Demographic Determinants of Spousal Marital Satisfaction." *Psychology Research and Behavior Management*, April 2016, Vol. 9, pp. 61–70.

CHAPTER 2: AUGUST 2008

31 **"Wilson Sonsini Goodrich & Rosati"**   Wilson Sonsini Goodrich & Rosati is an international law firm that was founded more than fifty years ago in Silicon Valley. Today it has sixteen offices globally, including one in San Diego, which was opened in 2004 and has an intellectual property focus. Peter was one of the associates who helped open that office.

37 **"Pythagorean theorem"**   A theory of Euclidean geometry having to do with the right triangle, that says the square of the hypotenuse (the side opposite the right angle) is equal to the sum of the squares of the other two sides. The theorem, as Peter explained to Evan and Anna that day, is written as: $a2 + b2 = c2$.

39 **"a cover band, Blackacre"**   In legal writing, *Blackacre* is a fictitious term used to describe a piece of land. If it's being used to distinguish one parcel of land from another, the second parcel is often designated as *Whiteacre*.

CHAPTER 5: DECEMBER 2014

69 **"the signs of addiction"**   According to the Mayo Clinic, signs of addiction—especially those related to the drugs Peter was using—include: failing to meet obligations and work responsibilities, lack of energy or motivation, weight loss or gain, red eyes, changes in behavior, secretive behavior, money problems, difficulty concentrating or remembering, slow reaction time, drowsiness, irritability or changes in mood, lack of inhibition, dizziness, falls, rambling speech, dilated pupils, anxiety, paranoia, nausea, impaired judgment, nasal congestion, mouth sores, tooth decay, depression, and insomnia.

CHAPTER 7: MAY 2015

84 **"I have Hashimoto's disease"**   Hashimoto's disease is an autoimmune disorder that can cause hypothyroidism or an underactive thy-

roid. With Hashimoto's, the body's immune system attacks its thyroid, damaging it so that it can't make enough thyroid hormones. One of the hallmarks of the condition is weight gain.

87 **"a prescription for Synthroid"**   Synthroid is the brand name for a drug used to treat an underactive thyroid—one that isn't able to make enough thyroxine, the thyroid hormone. Synthroid is the brand name for the generic FDA-approved drug levothyroxine sodium.

91 **"substance-induced mental disorders"**   The toxic effects of drugs can mimic mental illness and make it hard to distinguish them from an actual mental illness. These substance-induced disorders can include delirium, persistent dementia, amnestic disorders (loss of established memories and of the ability to create new ones), psychotic disorder, anxiety, depression, and sleep disorder.

94 **"angry and jacked-up"**   Childers, Linda. "Mary Forsberg Weiland & Bipolar Disorder," May 7, 2011, bphope website. https://www.bphope .com/my-story-rock-solid/.

CHAPTER 8: JULY 8–10, 2015

99 **"something called hematemesis"**   Walker, Kenneth H., Hall, Dallas W., and Hurst, John W. *Clinical Methods: The History, Physical, and Laboratory Examinations, Third Edition.* Boston: Butterworths, 1990.

PART II

CHAPTER 10: JULY 12, 2015

129 **"things he accumulated"**   Frank, Robert H. "How Not to Buy Happiness," *Daedalus,* Vol. 133, No. 1, 2004.

Quoidbach, Jordi, et al. "Money Giveth, Money Taketh Away: The Dual Effect of Wealth on Happiness," *Psychological Science,* Vol. 21, No. 6, June 2010, pp. 759–763.

129   **"craving sweets is a common"**   Contet, C., Kieffer, B. L, and Befort, K. "Mu Opioid Receptor: A Gateway to Drug Addiction," *Current Opinion in Neurobiology*, Vol. 14, No. 3, June 2004, pp. 370–378.

129   **"researchers speculate"**   Mysels, David J. and Sullivan, Maria A. "The Relationship Between Opioid and Sugar Intake: Review of Evidence and Clinical Applications," *Journal of Opioid Management*, Vol. 6, No. 6, Nov.–Dec. 2010, pp. 445–452.

134   **"any kind of lasting happiness"**   Richins, Marsha L. "When Wanting Is Better Than Having: Materialism, Transformation Expectations, and Product-Evoked Emotions in the Purchase Process," *Journal of Consumer Research*, Vol. 40, June 2013, pp. 1–18.

135   **"people at the top"**   Frank, Robert H. *Luxury Fever: Weighing the Cost of Excess*. Princeton, N.J.: Princeton University Press, 2010.

Frank, Robert H., et al. "Expenditure Cascades," *Review of Behavioral Economics*, Vol. 1, 2014, pp. 55–73.

Ganch, Brandon. "Work to the Grave: Choosing Consumption Over Freedom and Happiness." Dissertation. *Dartmouth College*, ProQuest LLC, 2014.

135   **"it's not just about consumption"**   Schor, Juliet. *The Overworked American*. New York: Basic Books, 1993, and *Plentitude: The New Economics of True Wealth*. New York: Penguin Press, 2010.

136   **"he contracted an infection"**   Endocarditis, the infection that killed Peter, is an infection of the inner lining of the heart (the endocardium). Bacteria can enter an intravenous drug user's bloodstream through unsterilized or contaminated needles and syringes. If it goes undiscovered and untreated as it did in Peter's case, it can permanently damage the heart and its valves. Another risk associated with endocarditis is that the bacteria growing on a heart valve—a mass called "vegetation"—can break off and travel through the

bloodstream to other organs, infecting them too. Without treatment, infective endocarditis is fatal.

McDonald, Jay R. "Acute Infective Endocarditis." *Infectious Disease Clinics of North America*, Sept. 2009, Vol. 23, No. 3, pp. 643–664.

Keeshin, S. W. and Feinberg, J. "Endocarditis as a Marker for New Epidemics of Injection Drug Use." *The American Journal of the Medical Sciences*, Dec. 2016, Vol. 352, No. 6, pp. 609–614.

145 **"our brains during REM"** National Institutes of Health, "What Is REM Sleep?"

145 **"psychiatrist Bessel van der Kolk wrote"** Van der Kolk, B. *The Body Keeps Score: Brain, Mind, and Body in the Healing of Trauma.* New York: Penguin Press, 2014.

145 **"a study they conducted"** Van der Kolk, B., et al. "A Randomized Clinical Trial of Eye Movement Desensitization and Reprocessing (EMDR), Fluoxetine, and Pill Placebo in the Treatment of Post-traumatic Stress Disorder: Treatment Effects and Long-Term Maintenance." *Journal of Clinical Psychiatry*, 2007, Vol. 68, No. 1, pp. 37–46.

CHAPTER 11: JULY 23, 2015

151 **"a DEA Report"** *DEA Intelligence Report,* May 2017. "Drug Slang Code Words," prepared by the Drug Enforcement Administration Houston Division, May 2017.

PART III
CHAPTER 12: BIG LAW'S BIG PROBLEMS

162 **"2014 analysis by CNN"** Flores, R. and Arce, Rose Marie. "Why are lawyers killing themselves?" CNN.com, Jan. 20, 2014.

163   **"at the firm Sidley Austin"**   Litt was critical of how the law firm Sidley Austin, her husband's employer, handled his suicide. In her *American Lawyer* essay she wrote: "Then came Sidley's handling of Gabe's suicide—'damage control' that included a last-minute invitation for me and my mom to attend a service at the firm. We went because I needed to see what kind of narrative they were creating. There were a handful of attorneys there, but in the immense receiving line of people who patiently waited to tell us about their unique story of Gabe, most were support staff. One told me that after working at the firm for years, Gabe was the only attorney to take the time to know her name. I heard story after story about Gabe's encouraging nature and how he made people feel like they could succeed at anything they put their mind to. One close colleague said she wished 'Gabe had his own Gabe.' "

Four days after Joanna Litt's essay was published—and a month after her husband's suicide—Sidley Austin issued this statement: "We have seen Joanna's letter in *The American Lawyer*. Her heartbreak is palpable and her words have moved us all. We have nothing but the utmost sympathy and compassion for the family as they grieve the incredibly tragic loss of Gabe. This is a painful reminder of the need to raise awareness and continue providing programs and services to help all lawyers and staff in addressing mental health issues."

167   **"law student health and well-being"**   Benjamin, G. Andrew H., et al. "The Role of Legal Education in Producing Psychological Distress Among Law Students and Lawyers." *American Bar Foundation Research Journal*, Spring 1986, Vol. 11, No. 2, pp. 225–252.

Benjamin, G. Andrew H., et al. "The Prevalence of Depression, Alcohol Abuse, and Cocaine Abuse Among United States Lawyers," *International Journal of Law and Psychiatry*, 1990, Vol. 13, pp. 233–246.

Krieger, Lawrence S. and Sheldon, Kennon M. "What Makes Lawyers Happy? A Data-Driven Prescription to Redefine Professional Success." *The George Washington Law Review*, Feb. 2015, Vol. 83, No. 2, pp. 554–627.

Krieger, Lawrence S. "What We're Not Telling Law Students—and Lawyers—That They Really Need to Know: Some Thoughts-in-Action Toward Revitalizing the Profession from Its Roots." Cleveland State University Cleveland-Marshall College of Law *Journal of Law and Health*, 1998–99, Vol. 13, No. 1, pp. 3–11.

167   **"Survey of Law Student"**   Organ, Jerome M., et al. "Suffering in Silence: The Survey of Law Student Well-Being and the Reluctance of Law Students to Seek Help for Substance Use and Mental Health Concerns." *Journal of Legal Education*, Autumn 2016, Vol. 66, No. 1, pp. 116–156.

167   **"Harvard Law School released"**   Results of the survey were published in an op-ed in *The Harvard Crimson* on March 29, 2018, "Wellness at the Law School: Promises to Keep and Miles to Go Before We Sleep," by Amanda H. Chan, Amanda M. Lee, and Adam P. Savitt.

169   **"a query on TopLawSchools.com"**   This is the query I posted on March 28, 2017, on TLS.com: "I'm a journalist who wrote 'The Lawyer, the Addict,' a story that ran in the NYT in July about my ex-husband, Peter, who was a high-flying partner in Wilson Sonsini (the Palo Alto–based firm) and who died in 2015 an IV drug addict. Almost everyone in his life missed the signs. The story wound up with enormous traction and generated threads of commentary on TLS, including this one: http://www.top-law-schools.com/forums/view topic.php?f=23&t=279754. I'm now writing a book based on that story for Random House. Although it is about what happened to Peter, the broader story is about the problem of substance use (and often abuse) in white-collar professions—especially law.

"I am hoping that some of you will be open to discussing with me what you see and what you've experienced in your profession and professional environment, in terms of drug use and/or abuse. I'd like to use some of your comments in the book and will not know or need to know your names, so I hope you'll feel comfortable being as candid as possible. I'm not here to make judgements, all I'm looking for is the truth about what's going on. I'm interested in whatever you can tell me about drugs you are using or observe being used in your field: which drugs, what effects you see, any stories you have, any details you can share. For anyone who wants to contact me directly, I have a secure and encrypted email through _____."

Responses to the TLS.com query can be found here:

www.top-law-schools.com/forums/viewtopic.php?f=23&t=287139#p10303333

169   **"ABA/Hazelden Betty Ford study"**   Krill, Patrick R., et al. "The Prevalence of Substance Use and Other Mental Health Concerns Among American Attorneys." *Journal of Addiction Medicine,* Jan/Feb 2016, Vol. 10, No. 1, pp. 46–52.

This study was conducted by the Hazelden Betty Ford Foundation and the American Bar Association Commission on Lawyer Assistance Programs, and is the most comprehensive study ever done on substance use and mental health in the legal profession. It found that 21 percent of licensed, employed attorneys qualified as problem drinkers, 28 percent struggle with some level of depression, and 19 percent with anxiety. Younger attorneys in the first ten years of practice had the highest incidence of these problems. Of the 12,825 attorneys surveyed across 19 states, only 3,419 chose to answer the questions about drug use.

170   **"Legal Professionals Program"**   This is the Hazelden Betty Ford Foundation's addiction treatment program specifically for attorneys, judges, and others in the legal profession.

171 **"anger, jealousy, and anxiety"**   Seligman, Martin E. P., et al. "Why Lawyers Are Unhappy." *Cardozo Law Review*, Nov. 2001, Vol. 23, No. 1, pp. 33–53.

172 **"experienced layoffs"**   *2016 Report on the State of the Legal Market*, from the Center for the Study of the Legal Profession at Georgetown University Law Center and Thomson Reuters Peer Monitor. The report stated that 2015 was the sixth consecutive year of flat demand in the legal market, weakening pricing power and falling productivity. The report also noted that since 2008, the law firm market "has changed in significant and fundamental ways."

   2018 Report on the State of the Legal Market, from the Center for the Study of the Legal Profession at Georgetown University Law Center, the Legal Executive Institute, and Thomson Reuters Peer Monitor.

CHAPTER 13: WHITE-COLLAR PILL POPPING

174 **"After probate concluded"**   Probate is the legal process through which assets of a deceased person are distributed to beneficiaries or heirs by an executor named in a will or a court-appointed administrator.

176 **"five stages of grief"**   Elisabeth Kübler-Ross defined five stages of grief—denial and isolation, anger, bargaining, depression, and acceptance—in her seminal book, *On Death and Dying*, published in 1969 by Collier Books.

179 **"volunteer at the Monarch School"**   The Monarch School in San Diego is the largest school in the nation for children impacted by homelessness. It provides education, emotional, physical, and psychological support; counseling; skills training; and so much more. The school is a nonprofit and relies heavily on private donations. To learn more about Monarch or to donate, please visit https://monarchschools.org.

180   **"White-Collar Pill Party"**   I reached out to Bruce Jackson, the author of that 1966 article, to see if he had any thoughts on how drug use by professionals and the economically well-off had changed from then until now. He told me via an email exchange in August 2018: "Some of it was indeed about weight [the use of amphetamines]. But that scene was far beyond body management. The people I wrote about in that article were talented and (so far as I knew) high-performing. They were using drugs I'd never heard the names of. It was fast, sexy, and apparently functional. I don't know what drove them. What drives anyone to get drunk night after night, or shoot up four times a day? The drug dealers in my days were guys on the streets. Now they're guys in offices."

181   **"more than 70,000 Americans died"**   "Provisional Drug Overdose Death Counts," Centers for Disease Control and Prevention, based on the twelve-month period from July 2017 to July 2018.

181   **"synthetic opioids like fentanyl"**   Sanger-Katz, Margot. "Bleak New Estimates in Drug Epidemic: A Record 72,000 Overdose Deaths in 2017." *The New York Times*, Aug. 15, 2018.

184   **"drugs of choice"**   Jacobs, Emma. "Illicit Pills for the Hyper-Competitive." *Financial Times*, June 18, 2015.

186   **"nine-year study of investment bankers"**   Michel, Alexandra. "Transcending Socialization: A Nine-Year Ethnography of the Body's Role in Organizational Control and Knowledge Workers' Transformation," *Administrative Science Quarterly*, Jan. 2012, Vol. 56, No. 3, pp. 325–368.

186   **"doctors are five times"**   Merlo, Lisa J. "Reasons for Misuse of Prescription Medication Among Physicians Undergoing Monitoring by a Physician Health Program." *Journal of Addiction Medicine*, 2013, Vol. 7, No. 5, pp. 349–353.

Karlamangla, Soumya. "Doctors and Drug Abuse: Why Addictions Can Be So Difficult." *Los Angeles Times*, July 24, 2017.

Berge, Keith H., et al. "Chemical Dependency and the Physician," *Mayo Clinic Proceedings*, July 2009, Vol. 84. No. 7, pp. 625–631.

187   **"about four million views"**   Estimate provided by Hacker News.

187   **"a large number of commenters"**   My query on Hacker News asked: "What can you tell me about drug use as a professional or in your profession? I know there is drug use in law, finance, medicine and technology, and am hoping that some of you will be open to discussing with me what you see and what you've experienced in your profession and professional environment. I'd like to use some of your comments in the book and will not know or need to know your names, so I hope you'll feel comfortable being as candid as possible. I'm not here to make judgements, all I'm looking for is the truth about what's going on.

"I'm interested in whatever you can tell me about drugs you are using or observe being used in your field: which drugs, what effects you see, any stories you have, any details you can share."

A link to many of the responses can be found here: https://news .ycombinator.com/item?id=16465762.

189   **"A 2017 State Department report"**   United States Department of State, Bureau of International Narcotics and Law Enforcement Affairs, *International Narcotics Control Strategy Report,* March 2017, Vol. 1.

190   **"766,000 new cocaine users"**   Substance Abuse and Mental Health Services Administration, *The CBHSQ Report: State Estimates of Past Year Cocaine Use Among Young Adults: 2014 and 2015,* December 2016.

190   **"an analysis of data"**   Bachhuber, Marcus A., et al. "Increasing Benzodiazepine Prescriptions and Overdose Mortality in the United States, 1996–2013." *American Journal of Public Health,* April 2016, Vol. 106, No. 4, pp. 686–688.

191   **"between 40 to 60 percent"**   Bierut, Laura J. "Genetic Vulnerability and Susceptibility to Substance Dependence." *Neuron,* Feb. 24, 2011, Vol. 69, No. 4, pp. 618–627.

Ducci, Francesca and Goldman, David. "The Genetic Basis of Addictive Disorders." *Psychiatric Clinics of North America,* June 2012, Vol. 35, No. 2, pp. 495–519.

191   **"both genetics and the environment"**   *Drug Facts: Genetics and Epigenetics of Addiction,* revised February 2016, a publication of the National Institute on Drug Abuse at the National Institutes of Health.

CHAPTER 14: BETTER LIVING THROUGH CHEMISTRY

194   **"this group spans"**   Williams, Alex. "Move Over, Millennials, Here Comes Generation Z." *The New York Times,* Sept. 18, 2015.

Dimock, Michael. "Defining Generations: Where Millennials End and Generation Z Begins." *Pew Research Center,* Jan. 17, 2019.

194   **"almost half of the U.S. population today"**   According to Nielsen, Gen Z is now 26 percent of the population. The Pew Research Center projects that Millennials will overtake Baby Boomers in 2019 as America's largest generation.

194   **"More than one in three"**   Fry, Richard. "Millennials Are the Largest Generation in the U.S. Labor Force." *Pew Research Center,* April, 11, 2018.

195   **"likely to be more troubled"**   Luthar, Suniya S., et al. "I Can, Therefore I Must: Fragility in the Upper-Middle Classes." *Development and Psychopathology,* Nov. 2013, Vol. 25, No. 402, pp. 1529–1549.

195   **"*Monitoring the Future* study"**   The annual *Monitoring the Future* survey has tracked national substance use among U.S. adolescents every year since 1975 for twelfth-grade students and since 1991 for eighth- and tenth-grade students. The survey is conducted by a team of research professors at the University of Michigan's Institute for Social Research and is funded under a series of competitive research grants from the National Institute on Drug Abuse, which is part of the National Institutes of Health.

196   **"Poverty and substance use"**   Ford, Jason A., et al. "Neighborhood Characteristics and Prescription Drug Misuse Among Adolescents: The Importance of Social Disorganization and Social Capital." *International Journal of Drug Policy*, Aug. 2017, Vol. 46, pp. 47–53.

196   **"Anxiety may be one reason"**   Wilson, Robin. "An Epidemic of Anguish: Overwhelmed by Demand for Mental-Health Care, Colleges Face Conflicts in Choosing How to Respond." *The Chronicle of Higher Education,* Fall 2015.

Denizet-Lewis, Benoit. "Why Are More American Teenagers Than Ever Suffering from Severe Anxiety?" *The New York Times,* Oct. 11, 2017.

The American College Health Association's National College Health Assessment, *Undergraduate Student Reference Group Executive Summary,* Fall 2016.

196   **"college students suffer from depression"**   American College Health Association's National College Health Assessment II: Reference Group Executive Summary Spring 2018. ACHA is an advocacy and leadership organization for college and university health located in Silver Spring, Maryland.

197   **"according to Twenge, 92 percent"**   Twenge, Jean M. and Campbell, Keith W. "Associations Between Screen Time and Lower Psychological Well-Being Among Children and Adolescents: Evidence from a Population-Based Study." *Preventive Medicine Reports,* Dec. 2018, Vol. 12, pp. 271–283.

197   **"major depressive episodes among teens"**   Twenge, Jean. M., et al. "Increases in Depressive Symptoms, Suicide-Related Outcomes, and Suicide Rates Among U.S. Adolescents After 2010 and Links to Increased New Media Screen Time." *Clinical Psychological Science,* 2018, Vol. 6, pp. 3–17.

198   **"child gets their first phone"**   "Kids & Tech: The Evolution of Today's

Digital Natives," published online by Influence Central, 2016. The report can be found here: http://influence-central.com/kids-tech-the-evolution-of-todays-digital-natives/.

198 **"40 percent of children"**   "Kids & Tech," report from Influence Central.

198 **"a 2018 research report"**   "The Digital Lives of Millennials and Gen Z: Consumer Research Assessing Gen Z and Millennials Around the World, When It Comes to Their Preferred Digital Behaviors, Habits, and Etiquette," a 2018 report from LivePerson, a company that develops digital messaging platforms and bots to handle customer service and e-commerce. Access the full report here: https://www.liveperson.com/resources/reports/digital-lives-of-millennials-genz/.

199 **"trying to cut back"**   Jiang, Jingjing. "How Teens and Parents Navigate Screen Time and Device Distractions," *Pew Research Center*, Aug. 22, 2018.

199 **"says Adam Alter"**   Alter was recorded in July 2018 on *The Art of Manliness*, Podcast #420: "What Makes Your Phone So Addictive & How to Take Back Your Life."

199 **"In her book, *Dosed*"**   Bell Barnett, Kaitlin. *Dosed: The Medication Generation Grows Up*. Boston: Beacon Press, 2012.

200 **"analysis of federal data"**   Carey, Benedict and Gebeloff, Robert. "Many People Taking Antidepressants Discover They Cannot Quit." *The New York Times*, April 7, 2018.

200 **"study published in December"**   Kafali, Nilay, et al. "Long-Run Trends in Antidepressant Use Among Youths After the FDA Black Box Warning." *Psychiatric Services*, published online Dec. 15, 2017. https://doi.org/10.1176/appi.ps.201700089.

200 **"in *The Wall Street Journal*"**   Sharpe, Katherine. "The Medication Generation." *The Wall Street Journal*, June 29, 2012.

202   **"a well-cited one published"**   Marshall, Paul, et al. "Effectiveness of Symptom Validity Measures in Identifying Cognitive and Behavioral Symptom Exaggeration in Adult Attention Deficit Hyperactivity Disorder." *The Clinical Neuropsychologist,* Sept. 13, 2010, Vol. 24, No. 7, pp. 1204–1237.

202   **"Paul Marshall, in an interview"**   Carroll, Linda. "Adults Who Claim to Have ADHD? 1 in 4 May Be Faking It." NBCnews.com, April 25, 2011. http://www.nbcnews.com/id/42710178/ns/health-addictions/t /adults-who-claim-have-adhd-may-be-faking-it/#.XNLYktNKiqA.

203   **"at low doses produces hallucinations"**   Hillhouse, Todd M. and Porter, Joseph H. "A Brief History of the Development of Antidepressant Drugs: From Monoamines to Glutamate." *Experimental and Clinical Psychopharmacology,* Feb. 2015, Vol. 23, No. 1, pp. 1–21.

204   **"FDA approved a new drug"**   FDA news release, "FDA Approves New Nasal Spray Medication for Treatment-Resistant Depression; Available Only at a Certified Doctor's Office or Clinic." March 5, 2019.

205   **"affected by exposure to"**   Mattson, Margaret E. "Emergency Department Visits Involving Attention Deficit/Hyperactivity Disorder Stimulant Medications." *The CBHSQ Report,* from SAMHSA, Jan. 2013.

205   **"the doses of amphetamines"**   According to the Substance Abuse and Mental Health Services Administration, the number of emergency department visits involving ADHD stimulant medications roughly doubled between 2005 and 2010, almost entirely among adults over age eighteen.

205   **"2017 article on psychostimulants"**   Urban, Kimberly R. and Gao, Wen-Jun. Mini review article: "Psychostimulants As Cognitive Enhancers in Adolescents: More Risk Than Reward?" *Frontiers in Public Health,* Sept. 26, 2017.

205   **"one in four young adults"**   McCarthy, Justin. "Snapshot: About One

in Four Young Adults Use Marijuana." Gallup Poll news alert, Aug. 15, 2018.

205 **"the brains of adolescents"** Orr, Catherine, et al. "Grey Matter Volume Differences Associated with Extremely Low Levels of Cannabis Use in Adolescence." *The Journal of Neuroscience*, Jan. 14, 2019, pp. 3375–17.

205 **"at around age fourteen"** As quoted in Nachbur, Jennifer, "Teen Brain Volume Changes with Small Amount of Cannabis Use, Study Finds," published on the University of Vermont Larner College of Medicine's news site.

206 **"marijuana samples seized"** ElSohly, Mahmoud A., et al. "Changes in Cannabis Potency Over the Last Two Decades (1995–2014)— Analysis of Current Data in the United States." *Biological Psychiatry*, April 2016, Vol. 79, No. 7, pp. 613–619.

207 **"*High Times* magazine ranked"** Escondido, Nico. "The Strongest Strains on Earth 2017." *High Times*, April 26, 2017.

207 **"Long-term use is"** Terry-McElrath, Yvonne M., et al. "Longitudinal Patterns of Marijuana Use Across Ages 18–50 in a U.S. National Sample: A Descriptive Examination of Predictors and Health Correlates of Repeated Measures Latent Class Membership." *Drug and Alcohol Dependence*, Feb. 1, 2017, Vol. 171, pp. 70–83.

207 **"2018 American Time Use Survey"** United States Department of Labor, Bureau of Labor Statistics, 2018 American Time Use Survey. Full results of the survey can be found here: https://www.bls.gov/tus/.

207 **"studies done back in 1993"** Kasser, Tim and Ryan, Richard M. "A Dark Side of the American Dream: Correlates of Financial Success as a Central Life Aspiration." *Journal of Personality and Social Psychology*, 1993, Vol. 65, No. 2, pp. 410–422.

208 **"testified before Congress"** Journalist Sam Quinones testified before the U.S. Senate Committee on Health, Education, Labor and Pensions on Jan. 9, 2018.

PART IV
CHAPTER 15: APRIL 2018

218   **"they also clamor for"**   The media has given a lot of coverage to Gen Z's desire for purpose and meaning in their work. A study done by Lovell Corporation in partnership with the University of Guelph also found this to be true. The report written about the study "How Millennials and Generation Z Are Redefining Work" is available on Lovell Corporation's website. Lovell is a youth market research consultancy based in Waterloo, Canada.

218   **"community is important"**   Francis, T. and Hoefel, F. "True Gen: Generation Z and Its Implications for Companies." McKinsey & Company, Nov. 2018.

218   **"pragmatic and they are hopeful"**   Allstate/Heartland Monitor Poll, Second Quarter 2015, Poll No. 23.

218   **"heart-wrenching essay"**   Chicurel, Judy. "When an Epidemic Is Personal." *The New York Times,* Oct. 7, 2017.

■ BIBLIOGRAPHY

Bell Barnett, Kaitlin. *Dosed: The Medication Generation Grows Up*. Boston: Beacon, 2012.

Brewer, Judson. *The Craving Mind: From Cigarettes to Smartphones to Love— Why We Get Hooked & How We Can Break Bad Habits*. New Haven, Conn.: Yale University Press, 2017.

Frank, Robert H. *Luxury Fever: Weighing the Cost of Excess*. Princeton, N.J.: Princeton University Press, 1999.

Giridharadas, Anand. *Winners Take All: The Elite Charade of Changing the World*. New York: Alfred A. Knopf, 2018.

Grinspoon, Peter. *Free Refills: A Doctor Confronts His Addiction*. New York: Hachette Books, 2016.

Hari, Johann. *Chasing the Scream: The First and Last Days of the War on Drugs*. New York: Bloomsbury, 2015.

Hinshaw, Stephen P. and Scheffler, Richard M. *The ADHD Explosion: Myths, Medication, Money, and Today's Push for Performance*. New York: Oxford University Press, 2014.

Jamison, Leslie. *The Recovering: Intoxication and Its Aftermath*. New York: Little, Brown and Company, 2018.

Lustig, Robert H. *The Hacking of the American Mind: The Science Behind the Corporate Takeover of Our Bodies and Brains*. New York: Avery, 2017.

Macy, Beth. *Dopesick: Dealers, Doctors, and the Drug Company That Addicted America*. New York: Little, Brown and Company, 2018.

Pfeffer, Jeffrey. *Dying for a Paycheck: How Modern Management Harms Employee Health and Company Performance—and What We Can Do About It*. New York: HarperBusiness, 2018.

Pollan, Michael. *How to Change Your Mind: What the New Science of Psychedelics Teaches Us About Consciousness, Dying, Addiction, Depression, and Transcendence*. New York: Penguin Press, 2018.

Quinones, Sam. *Dreamland: The True Tale of America's Opiate Epidemic*. New York: Bloomsbury Press, 2015.

Schor, Juliet. *The Overspent American: Why We Want What We Don't Need*. New York: Harper Perennial, 1999.

Sharpe, Katherine. *Coming of Age on Zoloft: How Antidepressants Cheered Us Up, Let Us Down, and Changed Who We Are*. New York: HarperCollins, 2012.

Van der Kolk, Bessel. *The Body Keeps Score: Brain, Mind, and Body in the Healing of Trauma*. New York: Penguin Books, 2014.

ABOUT THE AUTHOR

EILENE ZIMMERMAN has been a journalist for three decades, covering business, technology, and social issues for a wide array of national magazines and newspapers. She was a columnist for *The New York Times* Sunday Business section for six years and since 2004 has been a regular contributor to the newspaper. In 2017, Zimmerman also began pursuing a master's degree in social work. She lives in New York City.

eilenezimmerman.com
Twitter: @eilenez
Instagram: eilenezwriter

ABOUT THE TYPE

This book was set in Scala, a typeface designed by Martin
Majoor in 1991. It was originally designed for a music company in the Netherlands and then was published by the international type house FSI FontShop. Its distinctive extended
serifs add to the articulation of the letterforms to make it a
very readable typeface.